For The Love Of Darla

Barry J. Veden

ISBN: 1-4392-5778-7
ISBN-13: 9781439257784

To order additional copies, please contact us.
BookSurge
www.booksurge.com
1-866-308-6235
orders@booksurge.com

Dedicated to every lonely person, from Midwestern farming communities to Colorado ski lodges and beyond, who is looking for that special someone in their life.

The love you take is equal to the love you make
– The Beatles

Contents

Also by Barry J. Veden :

My Heroes (2004)
Coming of Age on the Appalachian Trail
(2007)

Acknowledgments:

Cover designed by Denise Moriarty

chapter I

SNOW-CAPPED MOUNTAINS rose majestically to the west, beckoning all within sight. One after another, as far as the eye could see, and surely beyond, the towering peaks rose like church spires pointing to heaven. The scenery was so breathtaking that the man viewing it could truly understand why his sister had relocated near the splendor that is the Rocky Mountains.

The lure of the high, rugged peaks and ski country charm has called many to its beauty and remoteness since American general and explorer Zebulon Pike encountered the eastern slope of the mountain chain two hundred years before, and had summoned Susanna when she but nineteen years old. She answered the call like a ship being lured by the wails of Lorelei, and remained until death stole her away and left her secret for a brother to discover.

Denver had taken the driver exiting Highway 25 onto Lincoln Street by surprise. The city was so much more than what he expected. True, it was a big city, but from what he had been told, it wasn't insanely big like New York or even Chicago. The city, for its size, with the possible exception of the traffic, had a small town flavor to it, one that was fairly comfortable for a country man like Charlie Wintergreen.

The weather was even more intriguing. It had snowed like the dickens in the mountains every day that Charlie had been in Colorado, but the snowfall the previous day was the first to descend on Denver since he'd been there. He had always believed that the capital city of Colorado experienced the same winter weather as the ski resorts in the high country. Now that he was there in the mile-high city, he knew that just wasn't true.

After spending a few weeks visiting the western city that sits on the very edge of the Rocky Mountains, he realized that the local media doesn't publicize that their weather is different than at the mountain ski resorts, and after talking to some residents, he realized they want to keep it that way.

"Let people back east think that we're all just cowboys and ski bums," they told him when he inquired about their reputation. "We believe we are the best kept secret west of the Mississippi, and we want to keep it that way. So don't you go spoiling it for us by telling people back home the truth about our weather." Charlie promised he wouldn't.

Hot coffee splashed out the top of a lid and onto his right hand as he attempted to make the turn without upsetting either the vehicle he was driving or the cup he was holding. The streets were clear of snow but wet and one-handed driving can be challenging in heavy traffic, even on dry pavement. Nonetheless, Charlie Wintergreen seldom went anywhere without coffee, and friends had jokingly remarked that his right hand would someday be formed permanently in the shape of a cup. He didn't care what was said. If drinking coffee and chewing tobacco were the only two bad habits he had in his life, he felt he was better off than most.

Glancing out the window of the rental car he was driving, the visitor saw block after block of stately brick houses on the busy street carrying traffic downtown, and wondered why anyone would want to live in a house that was so close to their neighbor that they could shake hands without either person leaving his home.

The houses on Lincoln Street heading to the business section of the city were built on lots so small that they looked like they were practically sitting on top of one another. They were beautiful and well-built, and expensive cars were parked out in front of them, but they were too close together for someone who had spent his entire life in a rural setting with few homes nearby. The area appeared to be one of the oldest parts of town, and from the looks of it, one of the most sought-after, but he couldn't imagine why anyone would want to live in a state as breathtakingly beautiful as Colorado and be that close to their neighbor. A feeling of claustrophobia crept into his psyche.

He wondered what kind of house his sister had lived in. He had visions of her on a ranch in the mountains, with horses in the barn, dogs and cats running free outside, and a lot of pretty flowers planted in the front yard. And the porch would have to be big enough to have a swing on it. Well, he would find out soon enough. He was on his way to the get-together with the attorney handling his sister's estate, and Charlie was more than a little apprehensive about the meeting.

The black Ford Explorer made its way through bumper-to-bumper traffic on the one-way street searching for the thoroughfare to the Federal Building where the meeting would take place. Charlie shook the splashed coffee off his right hand, finished what was left in the Styrofoam cup, and threw the empty container to the already cup-littered floor.

Charlie had spent all of his life in one place, pretty much doing one thing. The last few weeks had been amazing, seeing a new city and all, and he had a feeling the future was about to get even better. But he would never forgive himself for not looking for Susanna before she died. He felt like he should have found her before she passed, even if his mother and daddy hadn't wanted him to. He should have looked for his sister, but he didn't, and now she was gone.

Charlie knew that he would finally have some closure on his sister's death this day, and his heart was racing as fast as a wide-open throttle on his John Deere tractor as he drove to his rendezvous with destiny. His hands grasped the wheel tightly as traffic stopped for a red light, and while trying to pay strict attention to the task at hand, his mind was filled with thoughts of his childhood.

Susanna was Ms. Everything in high school—a four-year cheerleader who always dated the most popular guy, prom queen, straight-A student, a regular goody-goody type—but he never resented the attention she got while he toiled away in anonymity.

Charlie knew that his parents' farm would be his someday if he wanted it, and even at a young age, he realized that farming was what he was destined to do. He worked hard and learned as much as he could from his dad and from others in the country community. He didn't take much time to engage in the social activities that his sister and friends did, but he was all right with that; he wanted to be a successful farmer. That's what his life's goal was: farming.

Remembering their lives back when they were both still at home, Charlie was glad that Susanna was as popular as she was because she had to work so hard for their dad, and because he knew she wouldn't come back to the homestead after she went to college and began a career. She was made to do chores that were hard for a man, let alone a young girl, but she did everything she was told and never complained.

Susanna was really a good kid, and Charlie missed her so much after she left home. No one could believe that she just walked away without so much as a telephone call to let her family know that she was okay. Charlie always thought there was a fight or something that caused her to get mad at the entire family, but now, after her death, he didn't think he would ever find out what happened to her. She was gone, and both of their parents had died.

Charlie told his friends before leaving home, "I've always believed in fate, and I know that fate has a funny way about it at times; but I believe there is a reason for everything that happens. And as bad as it was to lose Susanna, there must be a reason for me to go to Denver."

A letter had arrived in the mail a few weeks earlier from an attorney by the name of Robert E. Sterling Esq., informing him of a will and requesting his presence at the reading of it. A lot of thought was given to the matter before Charlie decided that he would travel to the western city where his sister had spent most of her life since he last saw her.

Charlie had seldom traveled out of Indiana before, and when he did it was to purchase cattle or farm equipment in one of the neighboring states, so the thought of fighting a crowd at an airport and then getting on an airplane to fly clear across the country was something he had to give a lot of thought to. But he knew he had to discover more about his sister than what he knew, so he reluctantly made plans for the trip.

chapter 2

ON THE DAY before his meeting with the attorney in Denver, a storm moved across the Rockies and made Charlie wonder if the weather he had witnessed so far was an aberration.

People walking along a bare-tree-lined avenue in front of a deserted city park that day scurried for safety, heads bowed in an attempt to keep the harsh, westerly wind out of their faces. Among the walkers were a few fleece-clad runners on the streets and sidewalks, heading to Wash Park and its running trails, braving the elements as if they didn't exist.

The Washington Park neighborhood, or Wash Park as the locals called it, was situated fairly close to the downtown area where the attorney's office was, and that was one of the reasons Charlie rented a condo there. He wanted to do as little driving in the big city as possible. Some people referred to that area of town as South Denver, but Charlie hadn't traveled north of the business section yet so he didn't know if there was a North Denver or not and wasn't in any hurry to find out.

Watching the runners traversing the trails in the inclement weather, Charlie felt like they must be high on a latte or whatever else they serve in those new coffee shops that charge three bucks for a cup of something that tastes like the dregs of a hundred-year-old vat of molasses. He could get an entire breakfast for three dollars at the Comeback Inn, and the coffee there was drinkable. Three bucks a cup! At the rate Charlie drank coffee, he'd be visiting his cowhide wallet often if he frequented those businesses.

This was the type of weather he had been expecting to see upon his arrival in Denver and was prepared to see every day. Fortunately, the meeting with the attorney was scheduled for the next day, and as Charlie gazed out at the vicious wind blowing piles of snow up against the parked cars in front of the building, he was hoping that the streets would be passable by then.

The visitor from Indiana had met a young woman living in his building by the name of Ginny, and as he gazed at the weather outside the sliding glass door, he wondered if he would see her again before leaving for home. She had a tendency to talk way too much for a rural man's tastes and had a look in her eye that had already made him more than a little nervous; but he'd still like to see her again. She was about as pretty a lady as Charlie had ever met, and had a body that must be the envy of every woman who lived in the building where he was staying. He believed her biggest problem was that she'd been without a man for too long and was trying too hard to find one. And God knows Charlie had gone a long time without a woman. It sounded like the makings of a country and western song to him.

But he was sure that if they kept running into one another, he would eventually work up enough courage to ask her out. And then who knew what might happen after that.

The first time he saw her was his first day in the city, and as soon as her eyes fell on him, the dark-haired siren stopped the out-of-state-visitor in his tracks.

"You're new here, aren't you?" she asked as her hand landed tenderly on his arm and stayed. "I'm Virginia, but all my friends call me Ginny."

Charlie looked her up and down as if she was the most beautiful woman he had ever seen, and she undoubtedly was. After a few moments of stunned silence, he gently pulled his arm away from her and hid his weathered hands behind his back while occasionally looking at the floor and rocking back and forth on the heels of his new Justin boots, acting every bit the country rube he felt like at the moment.

When he did look at his new acquaintance, he saw a dark-haired petite woman with blemish-free olive skin, standing about as tall as his shoulders. She appeared to be in her early forties or maybe even late thirties. Charlie was never very good about figuring out people's ages and didn't even want to venture a guess as to what hers might be. Besides, it didn't matter how old she was; she was gorgeous.

She had a look about her that was different from any woman he had ever met, and she acted like she was his long-lost friend. Her look was one of confidence, but Charlie was thinking it was aggressive as he listened to her non-stop talking. Ginny wore a constant smile that showed pearly white teeth partially covered by lips that were full but turned up slightly on one corner of her mouth.

He thought her hair looked radiant, shining like the reflection of a million tiny candles as it reached down to her shoulders before softly falling over them. She was clad in an expensive-looking bright-colored suit that seemed to be custom made for her, and whose low-cut front showed an ample amount of her very large breasts, which he didn't mind taking a peek at now and again. Earrings dangled far from her lobes, and she wore diamonds on most of her fingers. Her nails were long and painted with high-gloss polish the same color as her lipstick and looked as if they also had diamonds embedded in them. On her feet was the latest style of footwear, which showed toenails painted the same color as her fingernails and lips.

He was nervously watching her as she looked him up and down; she stopped when she found his dark blues momentarily looking back at her. For a moment, his heart skipped a beat or two as they gazed intently at one another. She was drop-dead beautiful, and he was as jittery as a two-pecker bull in a pen full of Angus heifers.

Standing over six feet tall with boots on, the new resident of the high-rise building had to look down at the diminutive, well-dressed woman as she penetrated the forbidden zone that people keep around themselves when meeting strangers. They were about as close as a couple about to do a tango, and beads of sweat formed on his brow as he tried to dismiss his new acquaintance and her over-aggressive ways. The aroma of her perfume reached him before she did though, and it was a provocative fragrance that he would never forget.

"Yes, ma'am, I am," was all he managed to get out of his tightly pursed lips, and before he could elaborate,

Ginny started walking him down the hallway toward the indoor swimming pool. He followed clumsily, not knowing where she was leading him and wishing he were anywhere else but where he was at. His new acquaintance was talking the entire time, telling him how much she enjoyed swimming in the pool at nighttime when other residents were already asleep and wondering if he might join her for a swim some evening.

"You did bring swimming trunks with you, didn't you...uh, what did you say your name was, handsome?"

She stopped in front of the glass wall separating the hallway from the indoor pool and again was so close to him he could almost hear her heart beating.

No one had ever called him handsome before, and as if he wasn't nervous enough standing in front of this brazen beauty, his tongue was now so dry that it felt like it was cemented to the roof of his mouth as he tried to answer her. "Charlie Wintergreen," he replied, dried lips and thick tongue doing their best to spit the words out. "I'm from Indiana."

"Charlie," she said, stepping back and looking him over again. "I like the name Charlie. It sounds so ...outdoorsy and adventuresome."

She looked up admiringly at a somewhat tall, thin man in a blue plaid western shirt buttoned high around the tanned leathery skin of a slender but not gaunt neck. He was wearing highly polished silver-tipped boots mostly hidden under boot-cut, floor-length original Levis. A silver-buckled leather belt held the jeans in place around his narrow waist.

Brown and gray bushy eyebrows all but hid his deep-set narrow blue eyes, which appeared as if they had spent a lifetime squinting at bright sunshine. He looked every bit the outdoors type, with a rugged, chiseled face and a body hardened by long years of difficult work. He was physically fit and wore the look proudly.

"Are you married, Charlie?" she asked playfully as she cocked her head to one side and winked at him.

Mere minutes into the conversation and he was already more than a little uncomfortable in his new surroundings.

He had just met this woman a few minutes ago, and he was getting the feeling that she was coming on to him, wanting him to go swimming with her in the middle of the night and all. Then she asked if he was married, of all things. Charlie knew he had to get out of there before he said something really stupid.

"Listen, ma'am, I just arrived here today," he spit out hurriedly, his eyes darting back and forth between the woman and the uninhabited pool behind the glass partition next to them, "and I have a lot of unpacking to do and ..."

"Don't say another word, Charlie. I understand. But you have to promise me that you'll let me show you around the building the next time I see you. Okay? And maybe even go for a swim with me in the pool some night."

Cornered like a rat in his barn back home, the man didn't know how to respond to this catlike woman who was about to pounce on him, so he just nodded and smiled politely while slipping out of the arm hold she again had

on him. Then he quickly made his way to the front desk
and freedom. The scent from her body followed him as he
walked to the exit beyond the front door.

"See you later, Charlie," she cooed provocatively as
he neared the front of the building.

"The good Lord rising and the creek don't will," he
yelled over his shoulder as he stepped out into the sunshine, the words tumbling out of his mouth all jumbled
up so that they didn't make a bit of sense, and he knew it
immediately.

"Jesus Christmas!" He cursed out loud as he made
his way to the sidewalk in front of the building. "The good
Lord rising and the creek don't will. I couldn't even talk
right in front of that woman. Maybe it's just me not used
to being around someone that stunning, but I just acted
like the world's biggest fool. And that's probably who that
lovely lady believes she just met: a big fool. I think she was
just having fun at my expense, and I'm sure she'll have a
good laugh about it when she tells all of her friends about
the country hick she met today. The good Lord rising and
the creek don't will." He shook his head at his embarrassing faux pas as he looked around to see if anyone was wit-
nessing his rant. He would really be embarrassed if anyone
heard him talking to himself.

The single, middle-aged man seldom found himself
in embarrassing situations, mostly because he didn't allow
himself to be in a position where he could be embarrassed.
But this woman, this Ginny he just met, she triggered an
emotion that he had never felt. Call it embarrassment or ex-
citement, or whatever, but she pushed all the right buttons

to make him feel foolish. He wondered if his face was as red as it felt and if Ginny could tell what she did to him.

He instinctively reached for the round can in the back pocket of his jeans and, pulling the lid off, poked inside with his forefinger and thumb. A pinch of tobacco would be all he needed to calm him down. The yellow stain on his thumb and finger was testament to the frequency of his habit, and after depositing the mint-flavored tobacco in his lower lip, he unconsciously wiped his fingers on the back of his jeans. Loose bits of tobacco fell to the ground, but the stains that had colored his finger tips for so many years remained.

That encounter with Ginny made him jumpy each time he walked through the building he was temporarily calling home, and he made it a point to be on the lookout for the woman who made his heart flutter. It wasn't that he didn't want to see her. He thought about her often since that first encounter, usually during that time of night when you're lying in bed just before sleep arrives and carries your thoughts somewhere else. Who wouldn't want to look at a face as pretty as hers? But he was more than a little self-conscious about his inability to carry on a meaningful conversation and needed to work up more courage before facing that situation again. Besides, he couldn't swim and didn't want her to know that.

Sometimes, though, as he walked quickly to the exit, he would see Ginny coming out of the laundry room or fitness center and he would wave and say hi. He could smell her perfume even from a distance, and the aroma coming from that woman's body was enough to make him wilt like a thirsty flower in the heat of summer.

Ginny always looked like a movie star to him whether she was doing the laundry or working out on a treadmill, and she had a way about her unlike any woman he had ever met.

Coming from the fitness center, she would be typically outfitted in a gray workout bra that didn't seem nearly large enough to hold all it was supposed to, and matching spandex shorts that couldn't have been tighter if they had been painted on her taut behind. Even a plain old white towel draped around her neck looked sexy on her. She was beautiful no matter the situation and made him perspire even more than she was. She always wore a smile when she saw him, sweat or no sweat, and he wasn't certain if she was flirting with him or just being nice, but her actions were ego-inflating if not somewhat embarrassing, and he hoped she would never quit.

"When are we going for that midnight swim?" she would ask each time they met, a smile gracing her face as she cocked her head playfully to one side and winked at him.

He would just smile broadly while hurrying out the nearest door, avoiding gazing into her eyes and hoping the conversation wouldn't go any further. What would she think of him if he did get in the water with her some evening and never left the shallow end while she cavorted around the length of the pool? He didn't want to find out, so he just avoided answering the question.

Charlie had very little practice talking to women. He spent his entire life working long hours tending to the business of the farm and talking to men. He was usually up before dawn each day and typically worked till dark, sometimes longer during the planting and harvesting seasons. He seldom watched television other than the news and the farm report, and more often than not, he fell asleep in his recliner after supper dishes and other chores were finished. The man was a loner, had been most of his life, and figured that's how he would end up.

Men have a different language when talking to one another—kind of rough around the edges, like an oak plank coming out of a saw mill rather than the flowery phrases reserved for mixed company. What little social activities he engaged in were limited to church services on Sundays and occasional dinners at the homes of neighbors; and during those visits his language was brief and polite, especially on the Lord's Day. There wasn't much time for dating, even though he had occasionally gone out to dinner or a movie with a girl he knew from Grand River High while his parents were still alive. But she eventually married and left him to work on the big farm by himself, wondering what it would be like to have someone to hold and to share in his dull, nothing-special life.

There was always Brenda, a waitress in his favorite restaurant in Grand River, who flirted with him every time she saw him, but she had a houseful of kids, and Charlie didn't know if he could handle a built-in family so he never asked her out, satisfied instead to just talk to her each morning at the Comeback Inn. He thought about her from time to time, especially during the winter months when the field work was finished for the year, but his thoughts never turned into action.

Now, the day after the Indiana-type winter weather blasted through town, he was on his way to the attorney's office and the reading of his sister's will. He was nervous, both because of the traffic he was driving in and the unfamiliarity of the situation he was getting in to.

He found the street he was looking for and a parking spot nearby. After filling the parking meter with quarters, he took the tobacco can from his right rear pocket, opened the lid, pulled out a pinch, and neatly fit it into his lower lip, a maneuver that would be repeated many times this day. A fresh shot of nicotine would give him enough confidence to face the attorney and the legal matters being presented, although it wasn't courage that he was in short supply of, as over the course of his lifetime, he had weathered many a storm that would have felled a lesser person.

When both of his parents died in the same year, Charlie was left alone with a business to manage and life to live. And manage he did, despite losing the wisdom and sage advice that his father dispensed and the love and encouragement that his mother provided. He continued farming through both good times and bad, when crop prices were high and when rains seldom came, leaving him little to harvest in the fall, because that's the only life he knew. More than once, he thought about quitting the business and putting everything up for sale, but that's not what his dad and granddad did when faced with adversity, and he believed he was every bit the man they were.

The single farmer had been hurt seriously more than once while working on the farm and survived with only scars and a long list of stories that men share when they're standing at a bar with a foot resting on a brass railing while drinking a long-neck down.

He was bounced off a tractor he was using some years ago after hitting a half-hidden field stone at too high a speed, and a back tire of a wagon that was being pulled behind rolled over his leg. As a result, Charlie had to crawl for hours to get back home and call for help while the tractor and the wagon lay on their sides in a deep gulley. That was before cell phones were invented, but it wouldn't have mattered if they were around then because he was so averse to modern technology that he still didn't own a cell phone.

The doctor thought he might lose his leg as a result of the unfortunate accident because there had been so much nerve and muscle damage, but the leg healed over time, leaving him with a slight but noticeable limp and a newfound appreciation for cab-enclosed tractors.

A few years later, a case of pneumonia, acquired after spending a day rounding up cattle that bolted through an opened gate during a freezing rain storm, put him in the hospital for a week and behind in his work.

Charlie would later tell friends that those setbacks and others only made him stronger. His character was forged out of mishaps, he would say, misfortunes that made him believe he could accomplish anything he set his mind to, no matter the degree of difficulty. Yes, courage was something the man was endowed with a large dose of; but this was different. He was in a strange city meeting with an attorney about a bequest that he wished he wasn't getting. Even though he hadn't seen his sister since they were teens, he would have preferred she were still alive rather than him collecting an inheritance.

The streets were crowded as he returned the can to his back pocket, but not like he was expecting; and no one seemed to be in a hurry. There weren't even any car horns honking like he heard on his way through Indianapolis. The buildings were all taller than the one he was staying in, but he tried to avoid staring at them like he was some kind of tourist from out of town, despite the fact that he felt like that most of the time.

Unable to find the address he was looking for—there weren't any numbers visible on the outside of the tall, old-looking structures—Charlie stopped a passerby and asked for directions, expecting either an "I don't know" or a look of disdain as he hurried to a meeting or wherever it is city folks go.

"Sure, I know where that is," the young man in an expensive-looking blue pinstripe suit replied. "It's actually this building next to us, but you have to go around the corner to the right to enter the front door. There's security in the building as soon as you enter, and you'll have to show some form of identification."

"Thank you so much, sir," Charlie said, his southern Indiana accent probably sounding alien to the man on the street.

Charlie's gait had a spring to it as he entered the federal building and headed to his eagerly anticipated date with the future.

chapter 3

THE NOONDAY SUN was shining brightly as Ginny Wainwright walked the paved path at Wash Park deep in thought over recent events in her life. It was Saturday, and the walking and running trails were filled with people taking advantage of the break in the weather. A few miles west of where she welcomed the warmth of the day, tall peaks covered in winter's snow could be seen still surviving in the high altitude of the Rockies. But in the city, it was near spring like, and many Denver residents were out and about.

People with babies and residents walking their dogs were everywhere in the park, all of them seemingly at peace with the world. They all looked so happy, smiling and nodding in recognition as they passed Ginny, like everything in their world was okay. She recognized a few of those passing as frequent visitors to the park, and she smiled back or said hello and tried to act like everything was normal in her life, whatever the heck normal meant. Lately, it had meant walking in the park by herself and being envious of anyone who wasn't alone.

What is it about not being alone, even if it's only a pet you're with, that makes life a little more bearable? You can't tell your problems to a dog—well, some people probably do, but it's not as if the pet will offer you any advice in return. Most people don't want advice anyway. She didn't know of anyone who had ever taken the unsolicited advice of someone else, herself included. Maybe if she had followed the urgings of friends who warned her about the perils in her marriages, she wouldn't have found herself in the place she was today: twice divorced and alone. That was all water under the bridge now, and Ginny had tried to move forward with her life since her second failed marriage.

But she thought that it would be nice just to have someone or something to listen to her now and again. Maybe she should get a dog or seek out old friends, even if all of her past acquaintances were still married and would bore her to death with their tales of love and children. No, on second thought, those old friends would probably still be full of the "I told you so" that they all laid on her after her second divorce. She didn't need that in her life right now. She wasn't certain what she was in need of besides a little attention, but times had been hard since moving into the high-rise complex she currently resided in, and friends were hard to find. Maybe that new tenant in the condo could be that missing someone she needed in her life. But he was just a hick from back East and probably didn't have a dime to his name. Charlie, she thought was his name. Charlie something or other. Just a hick farm boy who seemed out-of-place in a big city. Still, she enjoyed teasing him and watching his face turn red.

Ginny was on a mission to find a man with money. There would be no more men walking out of her life, leaving her with only memories of love gone bad. Two rotten marriages were more than enough for any woman, and that's what Ginny had had to endure in her life so far. How could she have been foolish enough to fall for, and eventually marry, two guys who would go on to dump her for someone else? What was wrong with her? Was she that poor of a judge of character? Or maybe the men she had married weren't really in love with her after all.

She had been the perfect wife in both marriages—or at least she thought she had been. She was attractive, had a fantastic figure, and worked hard to keep it that way. She always dressed to the height of fashion and heeded her grandmother's advice that the secret to a successful marriage was to be a lady during the day and to be anything-goes sexy at night. Her men never lacked anything in their lives, sexual or otherwise, and repeatedly told her so. Yet they both left her for another woman. *What the hell is wrong with me?* she had asked herself many times.

Whatever the reason, she was determined that she would be the dumper the next time, and when she walked away from future marriages or relationships, it would be with all the money she could take with her. Love? Screw love. All she wanted from now on was wealth. And she was prepared to do whatever it took to obtain it.

"Ginny! Ginny Wainwright, is that you?" The dark-haired woman pushing a double stroller filled with two children stopped in front of her and stared in disbelief. "I haven't seen you since high school. How the heck are you?"

Ginny was startled back to reality, and it took her a minute to recognize Joanne as someone she went to high school with, and when she did recognize her, memories of better days flashed through her mind.

"Oh my God, Joanne, look at you. You are still gorgeous!"

They both laughed that embarrassing kind of chuckle that people do when they see someone that they haven't been around in a while, almost as if they're kind of, well, embarrassed that they lost track of one another over the years.

"Are those your children?" Ginny wanted to know, looking curiously at the two little blonde girls in the stroller.

"They're my grandchildren," Joanne replied.

"You're putting me on, right? I mean, after all, we're only ..."

"Too old to be having kids of our own," Joanne added before Ginny could reveal their ages. "I know you won't remember this, but I got pregnant while we were still in school and had a little girl that fall. You remember Derrick Littleton, don't you? He was the star basketball player on our team. Well, anyway, he was the father of my baby, and we were married right after graduation. A few months later, Gwen entered our lives."

"Are you still married to him?"

"Still married to the guy, but he doesn't look much like a basketball player these days. His hair is a little thinner, and his belly is a ...well, let's just say he doesn't look like he could dunk a basketball anymore. But he's been so good to me and Gwen, and now the grandchildren. I'm really lucky to have him in my life."

They both laughed, and Ginny bent down to get a closer look at the little girls who seemed to be taking in all the big girl talk going on around them.

"Hi there, you beautiful babies. What are their names?"

"The older one in the back is Jennifer, and the one in front is Megan. Aren't they just the cutest things?"

"They are adorable," Ginny said, smiling at the two of them as they looked curiously at her.

"Gwen had Jennifer when she was only eighteen—kind of took after her mom, if you know what I mean. Then she had Megan two years later. But I'm hoping Gwen's life will turn out as good as mine has been. She's married to a great guy, but they've been kind of down on their luck lately. We help them all we can.

"So, how about you? Do you live around here? Did you ever find that special person in your life?"

"I live in the condo across from the park, and I thought I found that special person—twice." Ginny looked at the ground as she spoke the word *twice*, and actually had to choke back the feeling that was swelling up inside of her.

"Oh, boy! You've been married twice, and divorced, too? How about kids?" Joanne wanted to know.

"I never did have any. But hey, that's all right. Single with no kids means I can come and go as I please. No strings attached to me."

Ginny didn't know why she was so embarrassed to talk about her life to Joanne. She hadn't done anything wrong, just hadn't found the right guy yet, that's all.

They continued their getting to re-know one another talk until both little girls got fussy and Joanne knew it was time to leave.

"I better run for now, but hey, I just live down the street over by Platt Park. Call me sometime, Ginny. And maybe we can do lunch."

"Sure. It was so nice seeing you again, Joanne."

Ginny watched her friend walk away, and that empty feeling crept back into her being again. Maybe it was envy this time, envy over a successful marriage and all the happiness that goes with it.

I wonder how many forty-year-olds have grandkids? Ginny thought as she resumed her walk by the lake. She now knew of at least one couple who did. Here Ginny was, middle-aged with no husband, no kids, and no money. She knew something had to change before she got much older.

Thoughts of babies and attentive husbands filled her mind as she looked out across the calm water in the lake. Geese and ducks were everywhere on the water, and some were on the shoreline, hoping for a handout. A host of people with small children were obliging them with bread crumbs and other treats, even though there were signs posted asking people not to feed the waterfowl.

That should be me with kids, she was thinking as she watched Joanne and her grandkids disappear across the street, and she wondered if having children might have saved her marriage, at least the first one. And if it had saved that one, there wouldn't have been jerk Number Two.

Ginny had married the most handsome man she had ever met when she was a senior at Denver University. At the time, she thought he loved her as much as she cared for him, and maybe he had initially.

Three years after they met, without even as much as an argument in their past, they plunged headfirst into marriage, and for the next five years, they were happily in love. Bill was everything Ginny had ever hoped for in a husband. He was good-looking and in great physical shape, and after college, he went to work at one of the better ski lodges in Breckenridge as a management trainee. He was a great ski instructor and eventually became manager of the lodge where he plied his trade. But more important, he treated Ginny like she was a goddess. They were never going to be rich, but they had everything they needed and most of what they wanted, and at that time, money just wasn't very important to either of them. Life was all about skiing and having fun.

But after a few years of that lifestyle, Bill decided that he wanted children more than anything, and when they discovered that Ginny couldn't have kids, the magic disappeared out of their marriage. At first it was just disappointment, but that soon turned to resentment and then they just stopped talking about it altogether. Then one day Bill came home from the resort and said that he had found someone else who he was in love with and didn't want to be married to Ginny anymore.

She was devastated and at first couldn't bring herself to even accept the thought of not being married to the love of her life. Then the reality set in that he had been seeing another woman behind her back, and she became angrier than she was hurt. The divorce wasn't contested, and each walked away without much more money or other material possessions than what they had in the beginning, which wasn't much at all. The main difference was that Bill walked into the arms of his lover while Ginny just walked away to loneliness.

A few years later, Number Two showed up; Ginny refused to call him by name. She referred to both of her exes by numbers. Number Two was all about partying; he had no desire for children, didn't take his job seriously enough for advancement, and openly flirted with every woman he came in contact with who was the least bit attractive. Still, she thought he would change after they were married. Instead, he only got worse. And then one day, just like Number One, he told her he wanted out of the marriage. Ginny couldn't wait to get rid of him, but life since then had not been good for her.

As she continued her walk around the manmade lake, her thoughts returned to Charlie. She decided she would have to find out more about him and knew just the person to ask. Bill, the maintenance man in the building, knew everyone who lived there. She was certain he could tell her all she might want to know about that Charlie guy from Indiana.

chapter 4

"CHARLIE, HOW COME you're so late this morning? Come over by the fireplace and tell us about your plans for the trip to Denver," a voice from the back of the room called out.

It was a few minutes after six on a dark winter morning in Indiana as he entered the Comeback Inn and Restaurant and made his way into the dimly lit but refreshingly warm eating area. Breakfast at the Comeback was a daily winter ritual that Charlie had engaged in for years.

The other boys were already there, sitting at their favorite table by the fireplace, lies flying faster than the snowflakes outside. The smell of freshly brewed coffee and the sounds of eggs and bacon sizzling on the grill greeted patrons as they entered the noise-filled room, and on this cold morning, the coffee smelled especially inviting.

The Comeback Inn and Restaurant had been a fixture in the one-stoplight town of Grand River for more than a century, and it showed its age. But the truth was it didn't look much worse than other public buildings in the town, and no one paid much attention to how a place looked. The Comeback was where you went for home-cooked, inexpensive food, to learn the news of the county, and, if you were Charlie Wintergreen, you went there just to be with someone. New ownership would probably spend the time and money to restore the old weather-worn building to its earlier respectability, but people wanting to own a run-down hotel and restaurant were in short supply, and the current owners either weren't interested in fixing it up or didn't want to spend the money.

Inside the restaurant, the dozen or so maple tables and chairs were chipped and nicked, and a few of the table legs had been replaced with others that didn't match. The cushioned seats at the six-stool counter were torn and patched, some of them tilting at such a radical angle that one wondered if people would fall off once they sat down. The tile flooring was so old and worn that no one knew for sure what color it once was.

On the walls, miniature steel tractors, the kind of toys popular in the early part of the twentieth century, were lined up on shelves next to the framed photos of past governors and presidents, including a very old and much yellowed photo of President Franklin D. Roosevelt. Miniature American flags were prominently displayed over every doorway, and Christmas lights hung in the windows all year long.

The fireplace was functional and always in use when it was needed, but the smoke from all those fires for so many years had blackened the field stone exterior and hung heavily in the air.

The entire inside of the restaurant looked like an early edition of the famed Cracker Barrel Restaurants found along the nation's interstate highways, the patrons that had traveled a lot had said, only not as nice. The main difference was that the Comeback was their slice of Americana, and they didn't have to share it with any outsiders.

The gravel parking lot alongside the restaurant was filled with pickup trucks that bore the emblems of American manufacturers, Fords and Chevy's mainly, most having seen better days but still functional. They were, after all, work trucks, and the men who owned them used them for what they were designed to do.

It was always the same faces at the two tables pushed together to accommodate the daily morning patrons. Once in a while, there would be one or two less, or one or two more, but mostly it was the same locals in the restaurant who had been making it the first stop on their winter day's routine for many years.

These were good people: middle-class, hardworking folks who were conservative in their thoughts and religion, probably more likely to donate money to the NRA than to some liberal give-away program. They went to church services each Sunday and to high school basketball games every Friday evening during the winter months. They raised their children to be respectful and honest, and for generations, those adult children stayed close to home and farmed.

Most of those gathered at the Comeback each morning were fourth- or fifth-generation rural residents, and some of them were coming to the realization that they might be the last members of their families who would continue the tradition begun by their forefathers many years earlier. Kids today were more interested in making money then staying on a farm working long hours with little reward, and their parents didn't really blame them if they wanted to move on to something more profitable. At least that's what they said publicly. In their hearts, the feeling seemed to be that the rural way of life that they'd known and loved all their lives might be disappearing from the American landscape forever, and they were all pretty morose about that.

All of the neighbors were proud of Charlie because he continued the family business started decades before, but without him ever marrying and having children, they knew that the Wintergreen name wouldn't continue much longer in Freedom County.

And even though there was still a lot of prime tillable acreage available for sale, or maybe because there was, there were rumors of a Japanese automaker looking to buy land for a new assembly plant in the area. "Country ain't country no more," they would all say when talking of the possibility of a large manufacturing plant being situated in their small corner of the world. Times were changing in rural America, and that subject was about talked to death every morning at the Comeback.

Charlie knew everyone in the restaurant. He knew them and their families; he knew of their good fortunes and of their illnesses, and found it ironic that the older they all got, the more they talked about their sickness as if that was the most important thing they had to discuss. Maybe for some it was. All the talk about health problems only made him feel older than he already felt. Everyone, it seemed, had his share of aches and pains, and on some mornings there was more medical information available at the restaurant then you would find in a doctor's office.

Maybe as their kids were all grown and moved away, and there wasn't much other news to discuss during the winter months, sickness was all there was to talk about, but he didn't engage in that conversation very often. Over the years, a favorite expression of his became, "Every day above ground is a good one."

The late arrival made his way to the big table filled with oversized coffee cups and faded plastic plates full of fried food and plopped down in the same chair he always sat in. The fireplace was showering the room with hot sparks from the new supply of oak logs recently thrown in, and in the background the AM radio station was airing an interview with the county extension officer.

The table was filled with older men in work clothes, baseball caps sitting atop thinning white or gray hair, all of them sitting in the same seats they always occupied as if they had their names permanently engraved on the backs. They all seemed to be talking at the same time, except for old LC, the most senior of the group at the table, who at ninety years old, still helped his sons and grandsons during the planting and harvesting seasons.

LC didn't talk very much anymore and didn't hear very well either. But he enjoyed breakfast at the restaurant and was a daily fixture there, someone who represented a connection to the past of Grand River, and everyone who ate at the Comeback held him in high esteem. He waved at Charlie as the late comer took his seat; he had known him since he was a boy and was proud of the work Charlie had accomplished on his parents' farm. Charlie acknowledged LC with a pat on the back and a "Howdy, young man!"

"You want your usual this morning, hon?" Brenda Morgan asked as she placed a cup of steaming hot coffee in front of Charlie.

He had known Brenda since she was a kid. She was cute, friendly, and more important, divorced. The girl had that rural look that some in the more urban high schools in the state sometimes referred to jokingly as "corn fed." She wasn't a big girl, just healthy looking, with broad shoulders enabling her to tackle hard, physical work, and wide hips designed for easier birthing of children. Having four kids in four years probably added to her physical appearance, but she was still appealing to all the single men who lived in Grand River and wasn't desperate for a man's attention. She was just the right size as far as Charlie was concerned, but he never told her that.

Her dish-water blonde hair always looked in need of a new dye job, but Brenda wore her hair in a ponytail, usually with a bright-colored scarf tied around it, because Charlie told her once, a long time ago, that he really liked the look on her. Her horn-rimmed glasses gave her a scholarly look and complimented her no-makeup, natural appearance. She had worked as a waitress at the restaurant since she graduated from high school and, like Charlie, knew everyone who ate there.

He often thought about asking her out to a movie or to dinner at a nicer place, but she was ten years younger than him and still had all those kids at home, and he didn't think she would accept. So he never asked. Forty seemed too old for a man to be asking out a thirty-year-old mother of four, even one who caused his heart to skip a beat or two.

Brenda, on the other hand, flirted with him every time she saw him, hoping that someday she would break down his insecurity around women and eventually—sooner rather than later, she hoped—ask her out on a date or just agree to have dinner at her house some evening. The single farmer would be the catch of the county, she told her friends, as everyone around town knew that he was as good a man as a woman could hope to wed. Besides, he was the owner of a lot of prime land and probably had more money in the bank than anyone else she knew. She even confided to a friend one time that the only thing she hadn't done yet to get Charlie's undivided attention was to serve him his breakfast while in the altogether, and if she thought for one minute it would get her a date with him, she'd do it.

"No, Brenda. I'll just have toast this morning with some of that homemade jam that you brought in."

"Okay, hon." She gave him a big smile, lightly touched his shoulder with her free hand, and headed for the kitchen to put in the order.

He watched her walk away until she was out of sight, eyeing her skin-tight jeans and enjoying the sexy way she had of moving her backside from side to side when she was walking as if she was warming up for a fast dance contest.

"Man, why don't you ask that woman out on a date? Everyone in the county can see her eyes light up when she's around you."

He didn't even answer the question, which had been asked of him many times. He felt it wasn't anybody's business but his own. Besides, if he asked her out and she said no, he would be devastated.

"Sorry to hear about you sister, Charlie," Jake Stevenson, one of the regulars seated at the table said. "How long's it been since Susanna left home?"

All eyes at the table were now on him as he squirmed in his seat, avoiding the questions they seemed to be asking.

"It seems like forever, Jake. I sure wish I knew what happened. She left home, and I stayed. I hope she found whatever it was she was looking for, but if she did, she never shared that with me or the folks."

Charlie always felt there was more to her disappearance than what he knew. Why would she leave and never call home? Maybe it was something he had done to make her mad. He had repeatedly asked his parents about his only sibling after she had left and they never gave him any answers. He believed they would have told him the truth some day, but they died before they had a chance to reveal the real reason she had stayed away so long, and he was left to imagine whatever he wanted to about her.

Brenda brought the order of toast to Charlie and lingered awhile; clearing dishes and moving the salt and pepper shakers back to the middle of the table.

Not wanting to get in her way, Charlie sat back in his chair and waited until she left, eyeing her close-enough-to-touch behind again before spreading the jam on his toast, but he couldn't help notice the smile on her face as she walked away. Maybe he ought to ask her out he thought as he watched her backside move even faster this time, as if Brenda knew he was looking at her.

Maybe someday I will.

"Why in the world would you want to go to a big city that you've never been to, and then stay there for a month?

I can just see you there, a certified country bumpkin in a big city. Are you a glutton for punishment?" Jake looked up from his breakfast as he spoke, a fork full of eggs and home fries poised in front of his mouth. A look of uncertainty filled his rotund face.

Jake was Charlie's best friend, and even though everyone else in town called him Ol' Triple, he was still Jake to Charlie.

The nickname Ol' Triple came about as a result of a hit Jake had in a sectional baseball game while they were still in school, one of the few times Jake put the bat on the ball all year, and his only extra-base hit. It helped his team advance to the semi-state playoffs. Baseball and basketball heroes in Indiana were idols in their hometowns forever.

Jake grew to be a big man as he approached middle-age, three hundred pounds big, but he could wrestle a full-grown stubborn steer twice his size out of a pen, up a ramp, and into a cattle hauler when no one else could. Three hundred pounds sounds like the man might be on the obese side, but he looked more like a rather large fire hydrant than he did fat. His short, stocky arms and legs looked out of place on his torso, but no one ever had the courage to tell him that. His friendly nature belied his strength, though, and even though he always had a kind word to say to those he liked, you didn't want to piss him off.

A few years earlier, because someone said something he thought was out of line, Jake picked up the front end of the man's car in the parking lot of the Comeback and moved the car sideways so that the owner couldn't leave the lot until other customers moved their trucks. Not many of his friends or rivals said things that might make him mad.

His short, dark hair, with sprinkles of gray mixed throughout, was always covered with a baseball cap, usually one that appeared to be too small for his big head, hiding the white strip of skin on his forehead that he proudly wore since he was a boy. Everyone who spends anytime in the outdoors and wears a cap everyday has such a strip of untanned skin at the top of his forehead and wears it like a badge of honor.

Jake's parents farmed on the same county road as the Wintergreen family, and the boys became friends before they even started grade school. They joined the Future Farmers of America as soon as they were eligible and remained pals all through school and beyond because they had the same interests and dreams. Their lives were filled with friendly competition concerning who could produce the most bushels per acre at harvest time each fall or show a prize bull at the county fair. Some years that would be Jake, but Charlie was the one guy in the county who seemed to get the most out of his land, and more often than not, he had the best crops each year. It was only luck, Jake would tell him, when his lifelong rival beat him. Just luck.

Seldom was there a harsh word ever spoken between them, but Jake liked to torment the hell out of his lifelong neighbor, and Charlie seemed to enjoy being teased by his best friend. Folks who knew them said they kind of fed off one another like they were always doing a standup comedy routine.

"I had to rent the condo that I'll be staying in for a minimum of a month," Charlie replied to his friend's question. "Maybe I won't end up staying there that long, but I've never been to Denver and I'd just like to see what a big city is like. Besides, I'd like to find out as much about Susanna's life as I can."

His friends were pretty excited for him because they knew he had never traveled anywhere. Jake told him he might not want to come back to the farm after seeing life in a big city.

"You know what they say, buddy. 'How you gonna keep 'em down on the farm after they've seen Paree?'"

"I ain't going to no Goddamn Paree, Jake. It's just Denver, and as soon as my business there is finished, I'm coming home."

Ol' Triple just laughed, as did everyone else in the restaurant, and told him not to worry about the farm and the small herd of animals that had to be fed and watered every day.

"Just go ahead and leave your friends in the cold and snow. That's okay; we'll manage somehow. Seriously, Charlie, you go to Denver and take care of Susanna's estate, and take your time coming back. You need to take this trip to find out what happened to your sister so you can have some peace of mind about it. I'll take care of everything for you here."

"Thanks, Jake. I knew I could depend on you for help. You know how much I appreciate you looking out for things for me, and I'll take care of you when I get back home."

"You won't to do anything of the kind, Charlie Wintergreen. You'd help me out if I asked you to, and you know you would. Just don't go getting on the wrong flight at the airport and ending up somewhere where it's nice and warm while we're freezing our butts off here. I would be mad at you then." Jake let out a big laugh, and soon everyone else in the restaurant joined in.

Ol' Triple and Charlie, they were a pair all right. "It's going to be mighty quiet around here at breakfast time till Charlie gets back from Denver," one of the waitresses was saying. "I just hope he comes back," Brenda said, and they all kind of nodded their heads like they were thinking the same thing.

Charlie still lived in the same small house he and his sister grew up in, such as it was. He could afford something bigger and better, but the house was on the same property as the farm he owned, and it was the land that was important, more so than the house. Besides, there were too many memories in the house to get rid of it, and he could almost see Jake's property from his back porch. He felt comfortable knowing that if he ever needed a hand with anything, help was close by.

The land, which now had almost one thousand acres of tillable ground, included a barn for the animals, several pole barns for his equipment, and other outer buildings. A house was just a place to sleep in and eat meals at, he reasoned, and living alone meant he had no one to please but himself. The old house was just fine.

chapter 5

"MR. WINTERGREEN, PLEASE come in and sit down."

Charlie had entered the office of Robert E. Sterling, Esq., the attorney handling his sister's estate. It was exactly 10:00 a.m. He shook hands with him, found his hands to be as small and soft as a woman's, and then anxiously gazed around the room.

Everything he saw looked expensive, especially the massive mahogany desk with a bronze sculpture of a bucking bronco on it. The walls were filled with framed diplomas, certificates, and photos of a man skiing down various slopes with majestic mountains in the background. Floor-to-ceiling shelves were filled with leather-bound books, and as Charlie stared at them, he wondered if anyone could possibly read that many books in a lifetime. The furniture featured plush leather chairs and the longest couch he had ever seen sitting between two tables decorated with sculptures of Indians on horseback. Everything in the office was as big as the view out the window, and he wondered if that would include the fee being charged to clients.

He seated himself in an oversized leather chair and suspiciously eyed the silver-haired man who was now standing behind the mammoth desk.

Sterling appeared to be in his sixties, or maybe older, but, like most people he had met in Denver, he was apparently a runner, skier, or aficionado of some other outdoor activity, as he looked physically fit.

The attorney was dressed in an expensive gray tailor-made suit with a bright blue, satin tie, and his appearance made him look like he could have been on the cover of GQ or some other fashion magazine. The few lawyers Charlie had any dealings with were more inclined to resemble an austere Abe Lincoln than the man standing in front of him now, and he felt a little more comfortable around them than he was feeling at the moment. He didn't even know for sure what the title *esquire* meant, but after spending only a few minutes with him, he thought if there was ever anyone who appeared destined to hold such a title, it was Sterling.

"Thank you, Mr. Wintergreen, for being here today for this very important reading of your sister's will."

"Please call me Charlie."

"All right then, Charlie. Before we get started, is there anything I can get you—coffee, water, a drink, perhaps?"

"No thank you, sir. I'd just like to get on with our business here."

"Well then, you should know a little about your sister. I believe the best way for you to find out about her is to read a letter she left for you. It's pretty important that you read this first."

A somewhat yellowed, sealed envelope with only Charlie's first name on it was handed to him, and he sat for a long time looking at it, turning it over again and again, before handing it back to the attorney standing in front of him.

"I think I would rather that you read it to me. Please, sir."

"If that's your wish. But please pay strict attention to what is being read. I imagine you will find it very informative."

After seating himself behind the dark mahogany desk, Sterling reached for a long, ivory-handled letter opener and slowly inserted the blade under the flap of the envelope.

With a deliberate, precise motion, he fed the blade the length of yellowed covering and in a moment it lay open, its contents still secreted away inside. Slowly reaching inside the envelope, Sterling pulled out a packet of papers about an inch thick and unfolded. Then he began reading the letter, annunciating each word with such deliberation that Charlie wondered if the man thought he was stupid and couldn't read for himself. Nonetheless, he was soon listening intently to each word that his sister had written.

Dear Charlie, the letter began. *If you're reading this, then I have gone to the place where Aunt Bonnie, Darla, and others are at. I hope that I'm reconciled with them as I miss them so much.*

It is the spring of 1995 as I write this, and I am still in mourning over the loss of my only child.

"Oh, my God," Charlie said in disbelief, and he repeated that phrase out loud again and again as the letter continued.

Did you know I had a baby, Charlie? Did mother ever tell you that I got pregnant in college and she and Daddy wouldn't let me come home? They were ashamed of me, and instead of letting me be surrounded by family and friends, they sent me away to have the baby all by myself. A nineteen-year-old girl, right off the farm, and that's how they treated me. I was scared to death.

I went to live with Aunt Bonnie, here in Denver, and she put me in touch with a charitable organization that offered to pay for all the bills associated with the childbirth if I gave the baby up to them. I knew Aunt Bonnie couldn't afford to help me out more than just let me live with her for a while, and I had nowhere else to turn. So I agreed to give the baby up for adoption. But when the time came for the agency to take her, I couldn't go through with it. Even though I signed papers, I changed my mind after Darla was born, and I kept her.

Charlie sat quietly in the plush leather chair, staring straight ahead as thoughts of his sister and her baby filled his mind.

He knew there was more to the story than just her leaving home. But after listening to his sister's letter, he wondered why his parents had kept Susanna's life a secret from him. Did they think Charlie might think less of her? Or maybe they thought he would try to help Susanna and her baby and leave them to mind the farm by themselves.

The letter continued: *She was so beautiful and so tiny. I couldn't just give her away. The people at the charity said they would sue me if I kept her and didn't pay back the cost of the doctor and the hospital. I told them I would pay somehow. And*

I did. It took me years to settle the bill with the agency, but they got every red cent they said I owed them. And in the meantime, I stayed with Aunt Bonnie and raised my baby.

In the beginning, I called home a few times, because I wanted you all to know about her. But no one would ever talk to me, so eventually, I stopped calling. I know you weren't to blame for what Mother and Daddy did to me, but didn't you ever want to see me again? Maybe you were poisoned against me and didn't care what happened.

Aunt Bonnie died when Darla was five years old and left her house to me, as she knew I didn't have anything and couldn't afford a place of my own. That was nice of her, wasn't it? She gave me a home to raise my daughter in when my own parents wouldn't even acknowledge that I was alive. I hope she was re-warded in heaven for all the nice things she did for me and Darla. I've remained in the house ever since she died, and I love the old place. I've never had any money to fix it up, and the Lord knows it needs plenty of work, but it's the only place we ever called home.

Soon after our aunt died, Darla came down sick, and not having any insurance, I couldn't afford the treatment she needed. So we struggled with her illness the best we could until the Lord must have figured she suffered enough and took her home. I was devastated, and I don't think I'll ever get over my baby dying. My world pretty much fell apart then. I lost my daughter and my aunt who watched over both of us.

Sterling stopped then and looked at the brother who was struggling to keep his composure.

Charlie had taken the can of tobacco out of his rear pocket, but instead of opening it, he was turning the round tin over and over in his hands as if he didn't know if he should chew in the lawyer's office or not. Bent over at the waist as if he was studying the carpet on the floor, he had a faraway look in his eyes. His daddy never showed any emotion in front of others when faced with a crisis, and Charlie was doing his best to be the man his father was.

Charlie always thought his mother and father were good, loving parents. But if they were, how could they have disowned Susanna at a time when she needed them most? There must have been a reason other than her having a baby. There had to be. But Charlie figured he would never know what that reason was now.

"Do you want me to stop for a while?" Sterling asked.

"No, sir, please keep reading."

The attorney continued.

I'm leaving you the house mainly because I don't know what else to do with it. Surely no one would buy it in the shape that it is in, and I don't have anyone else to leave it to but you. So the old place is yours to do with as you like. I'm sorry that you never had a chance to meet your niece. She was a special child who you would have loved. And I'm also sorry that we won't see each other again until we're in heaven, but I guess that's the way God wanted it to be.

Your sister, Susanna.

Sterling put the letter down then and looked coldly at Charlie, as if he was blaming him for what happened to his sister.

Ignoring the man staring at him, Charlie asked, "Sir, if my sister wrote that note in 1995, what's she been doing since then?"

"I really don't know a lot about Susanna, but in talking to one of her neighbors, I discovered she was somewhat reclusive after her daughter died. She had a job at a local branch of the library until she passed away but didn't engage in any social activities that her neighbors knew about. Most of the ones I spoke to didn't even know her last name. She kept to herself. Do you have any questions?"

"Well, what do I do next? Are there papers for me to sign?"

Sterling explained the technicalities of the will and suggested the paperwork be finalized before he left the office.

"Was there anything left in a savings or checking account to pay your fee, or do I owe you money?"

"No, I'm afraid there wasn't any money. I'll send you an invoice for my services."

"There's only one more thing. Do you know where my sister and niece are buried?"

Sterling gave Charlie directions to the cemetery, which was not far from the downtown area, and thanked him for being at the reading of his sister's will. He seemed to be in a hurry for the out-of-state visitor to leave, as if he was disgusted by his presence in the office.

"I don't know what may have happened between your sister and her family back in Indiana, but it's obvious by her letter that she wants you to do some work on the house. Whether you keep it or not is up to you, but maybe if you do decide to sell it, you could make a small donation to a charitable cause in her memory. I think that's the least you can do."

Charlie was enraged as he pulled out of the parking spot and into traffic. He was mad at himself for not looking for Susanna while she was still alive, furious with his parents for the way they treated their only daughter and grandchild, and deep-down saddened by the news of a niece that he had never met and would never know.

This was not the kind of news he was expecting to find when he left home. He didn't know what might be awaiting him, but he sure wasn't expecting this. He didn't think Susanna was wealthy or anything like that, and he surely didn't think he would be rich when he left Colorado to go back home, but he never felt poorer in his life than he was feeling that minute.

Walking across the emptiness of the cemetery, with its green grass covered with patches of snow, made Charlie think of fields back home just before winter wheat sprouts through the ground. Green sprouts poking out of the ground that time of the year are a sign of a new beginning for a planter of seed, with promises of greater things to come on the horizon. There were no such new beginnings or promises this day, only the hope of closure on a near lifetime of wondering about his sister.

When he finally located the place he was seeking, he saw two headstones marking the final resting places of Susanna and Darla, sitting close together as if planned in advance.

Susanna's marker was plain, only listing the dates she was born and died, and Charlie realized she was only twenty-four years old when her daughter died. He was looking at the burial site with tears in his eyes, still in disbelief that Susanna was gone.

As his gaze fell on Darla's marker and the sympathetic message engraved therein, Charlie experienced the most eerie feeling he had ever felt. He was standing only a few feet in front of the gravestone when he felt a sensation like someone was standing next to him. It almost felt like someone or something was brushing up against his body, touching him. Everyone has probably experienced something similar in their lifetime, maybe even more than once, but this was different; he could actually smell someone near him. He turned and half-heartedly looked around, not seeing anyone and awfully glad that he hadn't, yet the feeling persisted. Goose bumps broke out on his arms and legs as he looked at where Darla was buried, and the feeling became even more intense, like whoever was near him was closer still, almost breathing on him. There was a part of him that wanted to leave, but he was more interested in discovering what was happening, so he stayed and weathered the sensation. He didn't like the feeling very much, but he didn't want to turn and run like some school kid fleeing from a playground bully, even if no one was around to see him take flight.

"Darla, it's your Uncle Charlie," he spoke out loud while staring at the ground. "I know you don't know me, and I'm truly sorry that we never got to meet, but I'm here to pay my respects to you and your mother. I'm so sorry that life turned out the way it did for you and your mom. That's just not fair, and I know there isn't anything I can do for you now. But I'll never forget your memory, Darla. And before I leave to go back home, I promise that I will do something good in your name. I promise!"

Charlie turned to leave, tears running down his face, and as he did, he could have sworn he heard his name being called. He quickly spun around; expecting to see someone nearby, but he didn't see anyone or anything. It sure sounded like someone said, "Uncle Charlie."

"What is going on here?" he whispered as he stared at where Darla was buried. He knew he had felt something unusual, and he heard something too. How damn spooky was that? He reluctantly left the area, all the while looking over his shoulder to the spot he had just vacated. He wanted to see if anyone was either following him or standing by Darla's grave. The cemetery was still deserted, and he quickly made his way to the parked car. Charlie's head was spinning from everything that had happened to him that day.

First there was the meeting with the attorney, a person Charlie hoped he would never see again. Then there was the reading of his sister's letter, an occurrence that was even more difficult than the passing of both of his parents. Finally, this thing that happened to him at the cemetery. He was beginning to wonder if he had indeed done the right thing by showing up in Denver. What did it all mean? What did fate have in store for him next? A feeling of anxiety filled his body and mind as he drove back to his temporary residence by Wash Park.

chapter 6

RETURNING TO THE place he was now calling home, Charlie parked the rental car in the underground garage and entered the hallway deep in thought.

Not paying attention proved to be nearly disastrous as he tripped over Ginny, who was bent down in front of the doorway, petting a neighbor's miniature Dachshund. He fell heavily on top of her and the dog. The three of them all ended up sprawled on the carpeted floor, arms, legs, and paws in disarray. Keys flew out of his hands and bounced off a wall ten feet away. The dog was yelping loudly as its owner tried to untangle the threesome on the floor.

"Oh my God, are you all right?" He lay face down on the hallway floor with Ginny under him, her face inches away from Charlie's chest as he spoke to the seemingly inert body. She was wearing a look that he had never seen on anyone before, and for a moment he wondered if he had knocked her unconscious.

"Christ, Charlie, if you wanted to get on top of me, all you had to do was ask."

With that, she let out a laugh, and Charlie shot to his feet like he had landed on a bramble bush, his face as red as a ripe tomato. He didn't know if he should help her up or turn and run from the mad woman laughing at him. She sat up with her arms outstretched, waiting for a helping hand. Her black velvet skirt had ridden up high on her thighs, and the whiteness of her upper legs was exposed. She made no attempt to cover up, and he didn't ask her to.

"Give a lady a hand, will you?"

He reached out to her, grabbed her two soft-as-silk hands, and pulled her into his waiting arms, which she didn't seem to mind one bit. They stayed that way for what seemed like an eternity, bodies touching seductively until they almost melted into one another, the scent of her body and provocative perfume filling his nostrils and doing crazy things to his mind. Her breasts were pushing against him, and he could tell she was as excited about their close encounter as he was. His hands had moved to her waist, and he wrapped them around her midsection and pulled her even tighter to him. This was as close to a woman as Charlie had been in many, many years, and his knees were on the verge of buckling.

"I'm so sorry about what happened. I didn't see you or the dog when I came in the door."

The dog and its master had already departed, the owner with a knowing smile on her face, and the two of them were now alone. Neither of them moved from the grasp of the other. Charlie's eyes never left the woman he was holding, and nervousness was nowhere to be found.

"Maybe it was supposed to happen that way. You know what I mean?" Ginny asked. "For whatever reason,

I was going to be in your arms sooner or later and sooner happened quicker than either of us could have imagined. You didn't hurt me, and I'm enjoying the moment."

Charlie decided to seize the opportunity. "Can we go someplace and be alone? Some crazy things have happened to me today that I've just got to tell someone about."

"My place or yours?" And with that, she let out a little laugh that sounded to Charlie like she wasn't really trying to be funny at all.

Ginny could see that Charlie was pretty upset about something. "Sure, Charlie, I'll go with you wherever you want to go, unless it's back to Indiana. I don't think I'd make that trip today."

The two of them walked outside to the avenue in front of the building with Charlie thinking that someday they might both end up in her place or his, but for right now, he was happy just to have her by his side on a sidewalk next to a busy street in broad daylight.

He was just dying to tell somebody about what happened at the lawyer's office, and especially about what happened at the cemetery, but he wasn't sure what Ginny would think of him and his family if he told her everything he learned after talking to Sterling. She might turn around and run away as fast as she could. And if he told her about the strangeness at the cemetery, he knew she would leave him.

A look of concern was on his face as they strolled down the sidewalk side by side, destination undecided, while he wrestled with the thought of telling Ginny about his day. The beautiful woman next to him was giggling like a little girl on a playground, and the sounds of her laughter made him temporarily forget about all the badness he had experienced so far this day. Soon, though, he became a little uncomfortable with Ginny's giddiness, maybe because he had such important information to share with her that he thought that she was being too frivolous for the situation.

"Ginny, do you have any brothers or sisters?"

"Nope. I was an only child. Why do you ask?"

"I had a sister. It was just her and me and my mom and dad. Susanna was my sister's name. She left home after graduating from high school and enrolled at Indiana State University in Terre Haute. The day she walked out the door for college was the last time I ever saw her. And now she's dead. I can't even explain what I'm feeling right now. I'm truly at a loss for words."

"You just found out today that your sister died?"

"No, not really, but I attended a meeting at an attorney's office today regarding her estate, and I'm both mad and confused about what I learned about her life. I need to talk to someone about it. Would you be willing to let me unload my feelings on you? It's really personal, but I don't have anyone else here to talk to about it."

"Of course you can talk to me, Charlie. I'm a pretty good listener, and believe me, I've had more than my share of bad news in my lifetime."

They continued down the tree-lined avenue toward a row of small businesses as he considered how much information to share with Ginny.

Charlie wanted this moment to continue forever, yet he knew that he needed to somehow release all the anger that had been building up inside of him. He was in desperate need of a sympathetic ear and some friendly advice.

There would be time for other things later, but for right now, he wanted Ginny to listen to what he had to say and to maybe even offer suggestions as to what he should do with Susanna's property. Being from Denver, he figured she would have a good idea of property values in the city.

Tucked neatly into an assembly of stores on Alameda Street was a dog grooming business and a hair salon, sandwiched around a coffee shop that had too few parking spots. No one seemed to mind the lack of parking though, and patrons' cars, more often than not, ended up on the busy street out front. The shop was always crowded though, even if customers had to walk some distance to get there. That's where their walk led them to, and as they entered the business, Charlie was surprised at the amount of people inside.

He ordered a grande coffee of the day, while Ginny ordered some kind of a cocoa mocha something or other, costing Charlie a total of eight dollars, which he paid for without caring much about the price, and then they settled into a booth farthest away from the crowd filling the small room. A Dave Brubeck tune was playing in the background, and photos of jazz greats filled the walls. He was already beginning to feel more comfortable, both surrounded by a mass of people in the coffee shop, as well as being with Ginny. But he wondered if the people sitting around them would hamper the conversation.

"So tell me all about what happened today."

Ginny had moved her chair closer to him and put her hand on top of his and held tightly. She was watching his face, all contorted and worried, and was halfway to him with a kiss when he rocked back in his chair and started telling her what occurred at the attorney's office. When he realized he missed her lips heading his way, he almost lunged forward to meet them, then thought better of it and stayed back on the chair's hind legs. He was thinking about what he missed though, but first he wanted to take care of the business at hand. Hopefully there would be chances for other things later.

"As I said earlier, I met with the attorney handling my sister's estate this morning," he began. "It wasn't a very long meeting. Actually, I was the only one there beside Mr. Sterling, the attorney. That man made my skin crawl, and I couldn't wait to leave his office. Anyway, it didn't take long to read my sister's will."

"So did she leave you lots of money or lots of bills?"

"Actually, neither. I don't think she had very much to leave anyone."

"What did you get, then?"

"A house."

"What kind of house? Is it here in Denver? Do you know the street address? Maybe we can take a ride and look at it."

Charlie attempted to answer each question asked of him, but he couldn't get the words out faster than she was asking the questions.

"Actually, before I get to the house part of the meeting, I have to tell you what I learned about Susanna. I'm almost embarrassed to tell anyone what I just found out, and it about makes me sick to my stomach to have to repeat it."

"Go on, Charlie. You can tell me whatever it is that's on your mind."

The words came out of his mouth slowly and sorrowfully, like a preacher giving a eulogy at a funeral service.

"She was my parents' only daughter. How could they have just disowned her like they did?" he asked rhetorically after relating what his sister's letter had said.

"Why didn't they at least tell me about her situation? And after she had the baby and called to tell them, why did they continue to ignore not only their daughter but their only grandchild as well? I've always been so proud of my heritage, but now, after hearing what I just discovered, I'm ashamed of Mother and Daddy, and more important, of myself."

Charlie didn't reveal the incident at the cemetery. He didn't think Ginny would believe him and he didn't have a clue as to what really happened there. He would be hard pressed to tell anyone about it, even his best friend Jake.

Ginny sat quietly listening to the details of the meeting, realizing that the man across the table from her was mentally in a real bad place. She attempted to give him the support he needed to get past all the badness that had descended on him.

"I don't know the reason behind what happened any more than you do, but I know that it was all part of a master plan that we don't have any say in. I've often heard that bad things happen to good people, and I think this is one of those instances. I'm sorry for the misfortune in your life, but don't let it stop you from moving on. You have to get on with your life, Charlie, even if the pain is hard to endure for a while. Like everything else, it will pass in time." Her eyes were all misty as she spoke, her voice cracking with emotion. In the back of her mind, however, was the thought of the house that Charlie had inherited, and she wondered what she would have to do to get to know Charlie better.

He looked at the woman sitting next to him at the table and for the first time saw someone who seemed to care that his heart had been broken, someone who believed, as he did, in fate.

"I don't want to see my sister's house by myself. I don't even know if I have the desire to step foot inside. Will you go with me?"

"I told you once before, I'd go with you just about anywhere. Do you know where it is?"

"Sterling wrote down the directions for me. It's somewhere here in the city, but I don't think it is a very nice place."

"Let's go see it," Ginny yelled excitedly. "I don't know anyone else who ever inherited a house. How cool is that?"

She took the slip of paper and read the directions. "I know where this area is, and I think you'll be pleasantly surprised by it. It's not very far from here, and I can give you directions while you drive. Let's go."

During the trip to an area of the city known as the Highlands, they both talked of their lives.

Ginny was a widow, she lied. She said her husband died several years previously and had left her financially well-off—just how well-off, she didn't mention. She had no one to spend the money on but herself. Childless without any other living relatives nearby, her days were spent wishing that her husband was still alive. She never dated after her husband's untimely demise because she never found anyone she really wanted to be with. She looked at Charlie, wondering if he believed the tall tale she was telling.

"I've been awful lonely since my husband died, and it probably shows. I know I came on really strong to you when we first met, but there was something about you that drew me to you like a magnet. I feel like I've known you my whole life. I don't even know how you feel about me; maybe you'll tell me now. I think you are someone pretty special, and I believe we are being presented with an opportunity here to get to know each other better."

"I don't have much of a life to tell you about," Charlie began, "but I believe you're right when you said this may be an opportunity for us to get to know one another better.

"I've lived alone ever since my parents died. I have a farm in a small town called Grand River and have never been married. To be honest, I've always been kind of intimidated by women, and you about scared me all the way back to Indiana the first day I met you."

She just laughed at his remarks, as if remembering how he behaved that first day. She moved closer to him then, and with a sly smile on her flushed face, Ginny gently touched his cheek and moved his face slightly towards her so she could kiss him. Her kiss was warm and soft, unlike any kisses he had ever experienced before, and he about had an accident as his eyes left the road. He didn't realize that a woman's kiss could be so powerful.

"I could see in your face what I did to you, and after you bolted out the front door, I had a good laugh about it,"

Ginny said as their lips parted. "But I knew then that you were someone more special than any man I had ever met. And I was right. Boy was I right!"

The neighborhood they drove to was what realtors call 'in transition,' but it was a good evolution. Both sides of the streets were filled with old brick homes that were in various stages of need. Some were two-story original red brick, while others were one-story bungalows, some of which had been painted or even sided. Others had additions added on to them, and a few had new garages behind them. The houses that had been worked on were beautiful, some of them restored to their original condition, and gave one an idea of what a house in the neighborhood could look like after some attention had been paid to it.

At one time, probably around the turn of the twentieth century, they must have been some of the nicest homes one could own in the area, Ginny remarked. Over the years, the area moved through several cycles of upturn and down, she said. Currently there had been resurgence in the neighborhood as younger professional married couples were moving back from the suburbs.

In the middle of the residential community was a downtown featuring a variety of outdoor drinking and dining establishments. The area was filled with young couples strolling hand-in-hand, lazily investigating the myriad shops and restaurants. Ginny was energized by the presence of so much activity.

"Isn't this the coolest place, Charlie? Look at all the people here. I bet you've never seen anything like this in Indiana."

"Nope, I can't say that I have. It's the middle of the day. Doesn't anyone around here work for a living?"

Ginny just laughed at his comment as they continued searching for the address, and after traveling north for a few blocks on the street where Susanna lived, she saw the address they were seeking.

"There it is, on the left; you can barely see it behind the trees and bushes."

Charlie pulled the car over to the side of the street and looked to where Ginny was pointing. He saw his sister's house for the first time.

It was awful.

The whole house seemed to be leaning to each side of the middle and it appeared that every part of the outside was in need of repair. The roof was missing shingles, and the two brick chimneys looked like the bricks could use some mortar around them and were only in place on the roof because two metal rods were holding them there. The front porch had been enclosed, and the door leading to it was hanging loose from its hinges, ready to fall off at the first sign of wind. Trees and shrubs around the house had grown too tall, were too close to the house itself, and were in need of a trim. They almost obscured the view of the house from the street, and Charlie couldn't imagine what it must look like when everything was in bloom. Maybe it was best that he couldn't. Hanging in front of every window on both sides of the house were plastic milk cartons serving as bird feeders.

On each side of his sister's house was another that looked pretty similar and awfully close. The word, *claustrophobia*, came to mind again.

"Oh, my God!" he sighed under his breath. "I keep my animals in a barn that looks better than this house. This place can't be worth much."

His right hand instinctively found his rear pocket and can of chew. Taking a pinch of tobacco, he filled his bottom lip as he looked in disbelief at the house in front of him.

"This is even worse than I feared," he said as he continued surveying the rundown brick house. "I can't imagine my sister living in such a place."

"Let's go in. Maybe the house is full of treasures."

"I don't know. Maybe I should sell it for whatever it will bring and just leave it."

"Come on, Charlie! You can't sell it without seeing what's inside. Maybe there are things of value in there. Let's go in the house and just take a look around. We don't have to stay long if you don't want to."

Charlie reluctantly agreed to enter the house, but there was something about the place that made him tentative. It wasn't the appearance of the bungalow, although the brick structure was about as sorry looking as any house he had ever seen back East. He sensed something more, like some kind of danger, and for the life of him, he couldn't imagine what it could be. He reluctantly entered the house, but surely wouldn't have if he had been alone.

The front door opened with some difficulty—they had to hold the outer door in place and then gently move it aside—and after unlocking the inner door, they entered through a foyer, which led to a living room featuring a fireplace that might have been a focal point of the room at an earlier time. It looked as if it hadn't had a fire in it for sometime.

All of Susanna's furniture was still in place, including pictures on the wall of her daughter at various ages, one of them a large portrait that showed the young girl dressed in a floral print dress. For Charlie, it felt like an intrusion into someone else's life.

"This ain't right. We shouldn't be in here." Chills ran up and down his spine as he looked away from the photo of his niece. Maybe it was the thought of her dying and him not being around to help save her life, but something about that girl's photo gave him the creeps, and he was on the verge of leaving when Ginny stopped him.

"Charlie Wintergreen, you came all the way out here because your sister left you something in her will that she wanted you to have. You didn't know what it was at the time, but you came anyway. I don't know you well enough to possibly know what your motive was for coming to Denver, but here you are. Let's make the best of it and at least walk through the darn house and see how she lived. We can leave after that, I promise. But I think you owe it to your sister to see what she left you."

He knew she was right, but damn, he thought, this task was tougher than chiseling a one-hundred-acre field of clay that had sat unplowed for years.

The inside of the house was as small as the outside looked, and there was an unexplainable odor present, maybe because the house had been locked up for so long. It smelled like an unclean tavern on a Sunday morning. It wasn't a beer smell so much as it reeked from cigarettes and booze. He tried opening a window to let in fresh air, but each one refused to budge. Finally, in desperation, he let the front door stand wide open, hoping that the slight breeze moving outside would be enough to help air the place out.

The floor creaked as they walked into what was Susanna's bedroom, and they couldn't help but notice there were big slabs of paint peeling off the ceiling, ready to fall down on any unsuspecting visitor. Yellowed window shades were covering both windows, making the room dark and depressing. An old, dark bed and a dresser with a large mirror filled the small room. Ginny opened the door to the closet and noticed it was still filled with Susanna's clothing. Charlie couldn't get out of the room fast enough.

In the hallway separating the two bedrooms, the only bathroom was so small that it was hard to envision two people being in it at one time. Inside both the sink and bathtub, there was a line of rust from the dripping coming out of the faucets. The pink curtain hanging from the window was so dirty that it appeared more charcoal-colored than it did a shade of red. The bathroom didn't appear to be a place one would want to enter to get clean.

"The entire house needs a thorough cleaning," Ginny said. "But I bet when it's spruced up some, it would really be nice."

Charlie just looked at her as if she was crazy but didn't say anything.

Opening a closed door into the other bedroom at the end of the narrow hallway, they saw an infant's bed filled with lots of colorful stuffed animals pushed back into one corner of the room, mute testimony to who had once slept there. On the walls were pictures of small cuddly animals in pink frames, and one black and white photo of the Wintergreen farm in Indiana, taken when Susanna was a small girl.

The chest of drawers had a vintage black and white photo on top of it and, looking closer, they saw it was a childhood photo of Susanna and her brother, with the words, "Uncle Charlie" inked on the glass. He felt a big lump in his throat at the sight of the photo, knowing that Susanna must have told her daughter about him. The room looked like a child was still living there despite his niece having died years earlier.

"It looks like no one ever entered this room again after Darla died," Charlie remarked as he nervously scanned the child's bedroom.

"I've heard of people doing that after losing a child. It's like they think their loved one might return someday, and they want to keep everything the same for their arrival," Ginny said while trying not to sound too disrespectful of Charlie's sister.

"This is way too weird for me. I just don't feel right being here. What am I going to do with this place?"

"Why don't we try to fix it up?"

There was a long pause as Charlie stared at Ginny.

"*We?* You mean you and me?"

She was standing close to him now, her eyes firmly fixed on his. That turned-up smile was on her face, and her eyes sparkled as she folded her arms in front of her chest and answered him.

"Sure! Why not?" Confidence was bubbling out of Ginny as she spoke. "We could remodel it so it looks like someplace we, uh, you, or someone else, would want to live in. I just love the area, don't you?"

He didn't answer her for a while, thinking about what he was going to say. When he finally did respond, he said, "I appreciate what you seem to be offering me, but have you ever done physical work in your life? Do you have any idea what we could be getting into here? I mean, this place will take lots of work, and then, even if we did that, I don't know if it would turn out nice enough to live in or even to sell. I mean ...look at this place. Do you really have a vision of what it could look like when we're finished with it?"

"I just know that we can make it look better than what it does right now. Maybe we wouldn't actually have to do the work ourselves. We could hire contractors and just oversee their work."

"Yeah, maybe. But I could probably do most of the work on the house, especially the demolition part of it. I'm pretty handy with tools. But it would take months to finish, and I have a farm back home. I don't know if it's a project that I want to tackle."

"C'mon, Charlie. You wouldn't be doing it all by yourself, you know. I don't have anything else going on in my life, and I'm willing to help you all that I can. Besides, I think it would be a fun project, and it would mean we could spend some time together. What do you say?"

He realized it might be a way to get to know this beautiful woman he was taking a liking to, and the idea was appealing, but there were many other aspects to take into consideration, not the least of which was asking his buddy Jake for help. Then there was that unexplainable occurrence at the cemetery and the uneasy feeling he experienced when they first entered the house. He didn't know what to make of either of the incidents and didn't know if the uncomfortable feeling would ever go away, but he didn't want to tell Ginny about it, either. She might wonder what she got herself into if he told her he was kind of afraid of what might be in the house.

"I'll have to call my friend first and see if he can sell off the cattle that I have so that he doesn't have to tend to them every day. Let me call him before I make any decisions, okay?"

"Well I don't think we have to make any decisions today, but you should consider fixing the place up. That's just my personal feeling. You do whatever you believe is right for you. I want you to know, though, that if you decide to sell the house and go back home, I'll understand. For purely selfish reasons, I hope you won't do that, but if that's your decision, I'll understand." She laid her head against his shoulder as they stood side by side, looking at Susanna's house, both of them deep in thought about the possibilities.

Charlie felt like this might the chance he was seeking to spend more time with Ginny, and the idea of fixing up Susanna's house was attractive to him. He knew it would take some effort to fix the house so it could be sold but thought maybe this is why he was in Denver: to do something in Susanna's memory. He decided to call Jake in the morning and see if he would be willing to sell the cattle for Charlie.

Ginny, meanwhile, was thinking that this might be her opportunity to finally come into some money.

chapter 7

THE VIEW LOOKING from the balcony to the west was incredible in the daylight, for in the early morning light before the sun rose fully, the tall peaks looked purple and gray and distant; and when the noonday sun splashed bright colors over them, the mountains took on the hues of an artist's palette and appeared closer. He was hoping to still be able to see them now, but the tall peaks were lost to the dark of night, and he couldn't.

There was something exciting about living so close to the rocky heights, Charlie had told his friends back in Indiana, maybe because he had been a flatlander all of his life.

The closest he had ever been to a mountain previously was when he was a boy on a trip to the Indiana Dunes along the Lake Michigan shoreline, but the dunes were sand and not very tall, although at the time, they felt like mountains to him. He climbed to the top of Mount Baldy, naked of any vegetation, on the wind-swept shoreline of the Indiana side of the big lake, and saw the city of Chicago across the water rising like the legendary Phoenix.

The Rockies were real mountains, tall and hard and full of life. They were close enough to the city that he felt like he could reach out and touch them anytime he wanted, and the Midwesterner gazed at them frequently, wistfully wondering how he could spend more time in the high country, upset because he hadn't done that yet. It was like they were calling to him to visit and explore and discover, and he wasn't. Maybe that's where fate was directing him, Charlie thought, to the mountains.

He sat on a folding chair outside the sliding glass door of his twentieth floor rental unit, staring at the sky full of bright stars, contemplating the events of the last few hours. Across the city, with its bright lights and tall buildings, a cool breeze blew from the northwest and made the temperature chilly enough to make him remember it wasn't quite spring, but not cold enough to think of winter back home. He sat outside dressed in only a robe, drinking a freshly brewed cup of coffee. He wouldn't be sitting outside dressed like this if he was at the farm, and he would probably already be in bed, alone. Alone was all there was in Charlie's life, and although he would never admit it to anyone, he was tired of living that way.

Inside lay the most beautiful woman he had ever known. He had made love with her until he couldn't love anymore, and still she wouldn't let him go. She was incredible in bed, and they held onto each other afterwards, lust-filled bodies sated, as if each was afraid the other might disappear forever. Ginny told him over and over he was an incredible lover, asking him to never leave her side. He held her that way, arms and legs intertwined, hot breath not yet abated, saying nothing to her other than the under-ones-breath words that people say when they are in the throes of lovemaking. The word *love* was never mentioned by either of them, though, because at this early point in their relationship, it was only desire that brought them together with no promise that anything more enduring might follow. For now, that was enough for Charlie.

When he was certain she was asleep, he slipped out from underneath the covers and left the bedroom to ponder his future.

Charlie stared out across the city that was still full of life, even in the middle of the night, and thought about all that had happened to him since being in Colorado.

In the background, a siren could be heard as fire trucks from a nearby station left to answer a call for help, and somewhere nearby a motorcycle roared through the city, the blare from its muffler bouncing off the tall buildings, making the motor seem louder than it already was.

In a few short days, Charlie had discovered the truth about his sister's disappearance, found out that he had a niece who died, inherited a house in need of much repair work, and met a woman that he just took to bed. To a guy who has led a pretty dull, nothing-special life, each was an earth-shattering event rife with ramifications far beyond the obvious and required some serious soul searching.

He knew that he couldn't stay in Denver and take on the remodeling project without completely altering his lifestyle. Farming was all he knew how to do. Yet there was a part of him that didn't want to leave, and despite the strange feelings he experienced at the cemetery and when they entered Susanna's home, working on his sister's house might be a way to satisfy his desire to do something in her memory and continue the relationship-building with the beautiful woman in his bedroom.

The man was at a crossroads in his life, perhaps the first real one that he ever encountered, and wasn't certain which path he should take. One road led back home to the same boring life he knew from before, but it was one that he knew how to manage.

Waiting for him on the farm would be hour after hour of hard work, day after day, three seasons of the year, without any guarantee of success, but with the satisfaction that comes at the end of the day when you step out of your tractor knowing that you have put in a good day's effort. That was a life he had known since he was a boy and was fully capable of continuing. The other part waiting for him at home, and perhaps the most important, was a comfortable life. There's something to be said about being comfortable in life, he thought, especially at his age.

The other road he could take, although filled with challenges, offered more opportunities and the distinct possibility of love.

For a man who had never known love, the thought of it was now in his mind every waking minute. He was beginning to understand how other people, maybe even his sister, could become so overwhelmed by the need to love and be loved that it consumed them, much like was happening to him now. He couldn't have imagined just a few short weeks ago that his mind would be filled with thoughts of a woman, but he had definitely been bitten by whatever kind of bug causes a man to feel this way, and he was both enjoying and fearing the new feeling. Deep down, he also knew that the path that led to Ginny had a bigger chance of failure, and he didn't take to failure very well.

He held the cup of steaming hot coffee between both hands as if the heat from the cup would keep him warm, even though it wasn't, and thought about calling his friend at home.

Charlie was certain that Jake would know what he should do; at least he would listen to him with a sympathetic ear and offer advice that he believed would be in Charlie's best interest. Jake always had good suggestion to offer. All he would have to do was sell the cattle. The farm and its equipment would be all right for awhile. Actual work in the fields wouldn't be starting for another five or six weeks, so there was plenty of time to finish the house and get back home in time for the planting season. He decided to call Jake in the morning.

After leaving the Highlands area earlier, Charlie and Ginny decided to have dinner and continue the discussion about Susanna's house while dining on a nice meal. She suggested a sushi bar on Pearl Street as a possibility, but Charlie was a cattleman and lover of beef. If dinner didn't include meat and potatoes, he told her, it wasn't fit to eat.

They stopped at the finest steak house in town for dinner and drinks, and were soon saying all the things to one another that a man and woman say when they're having their first meal together and enjoying each other's company. The initial conversation concerned the house and what it would take to fix it up.

Charlie was more interested in subtracting the parts that he believed were unfixable, while Ginny seemed to be more focused on taking what was left afterward and restoring it to its original condition.

"We've just got to take down that old garage out in back and the add-on enclosed porch. Neither one of them fit the house, and I think it would make a huge difference with them gone," Charlie remarked. "We can hire someone to build a new garage and to replace that old furnace after I remove it from the basement. I think that's where we should start."

"Well while you're doing the demo work on the garage and back porch, I can start stripping the old wallpaper off the walls and taking up the carpet," Ginny said. "I'm anxious to see what's lurking under all that wallpaper and nasty-looking carpet in the house. I'll bet there are beautiful hardwood floors that can be restored and give the whole place a new look."

"I agree, but the floors can come later. Let's first concentrate on the walls and ceiling, and replacing the other items that need to be replaced."

"Yeah, like that nasty sink and tub in the bathroom."

"Do you know any contractors who we could contact?" Charlie wanted to know.

"I don't personally, but I know a guy who could probably give us the names of some people in the business."

"Great! I can't wait to get started."

The longer the discussion continued, the more he realized that they would make a good team. A few drinks led to a few more, and then the conversation meandered more toward the personal side. Before he knew it, the discussion had taken a definite romantic turn.

"Let me ask you something, Charlie," Ginny said before leaving the restaurant. "Do you find me attractive?"

"You're kidding me, right?"

"No. I'm not kidding, Charlie. I want to know if I'm someone you want to be with."

"Ginny, you are the most beautiful and desirable woman I've ever met. I want to be with you more than anything else I can think of. Maybe I don't show my emotions as much as you would like, but trust me when I tell you that you are definitely someone I want to be with."

Charlie moved his chair around the table until he was next to Ginny and put his arms around her.

"Let's get out of here," he whispered in her ear.

"Your place or mine?" she answered, and with that, they both laughed.

He didn't even remember how big of a tip was left at the table—too big probably—because they were in such a hurry to be somewhere else.

Once inside the condo by the park and alone in the elevator, a feverish first kiss led to the taking off of one another's clothes—actually, more unbuttoning and unzipping than taking off. But by the time the slow-moving elevator arrived at the top floor of the building, they might as well have been naked. She was making so much passionate noise that Charlie was afraid the neighbors might hear them, and he told her so. She didn't care, she said, who heard them. He picked her up at the doorway to his unit and carried her to the bedroom.

Charlie didn't know that a woman could make him feel what he was feeling, he thought, as he continued drinking the hot coffee on the deck outside the sliding glass doors while reminiscing about the romantic interlude earlier.

He knew it wasn't just the sex, although that was pretty damn good. Charlie was beginning to realize that he wanted to be with her more than he wanted to be with anyone else in his life. Ginny said and did all the right things to make him feel important. He had never felt that way about anyone in his life and figured if that is what love was like, he wanted more of it. He knew that he couldn't just walk away from Ginny. Besides, he really didn't want to be away from her.

First there was a phone call that had to be made to the only person he trusted. That would come in the morning. Right now, there was a beautiful woman in his bed, and he wanted to be there with her.

chapter 8

THEY STOOD ON the sidewalk and watched the big truck unload the roll-off in front of Susanna's house, and they knew the journey had begun. Where it would end was an item they hadn't spent a lot of time talking about yet. They stood there like hired hands reporting for work on the first day of the job, alternating their pensive looks between the disastrous-looking house on the lot and the empty roll-off in the street, wondering if they really did want to begin the monumental task. The house renovation was staring them in the face, yet they didn't know how to begin. It was as if they were both toeing a chalk line, waiting for the starter's pistol to be fired or for someone to yell, "On your mark, get set, go!"

Actually, there was a plan that called for a beginning, but anyone can plan something; implementing it, however, is usually another story.

The last two weeks had been hectic, as there was much that needed to be accomplished before the actual work could begin. First there were remodeling plans to submit to the city and permits to obtain. Ginny worked with Charlie every day on the plans, offering suggestions for improvements and even obtaining the permits, because she knew her way around town better than he did, and her smile and friendly ways seemed to get more accomplished than he could have. Her good looks didn't hurt, either.

The business at hand didn't interfere with the relationship, and every evening was spent together dining out. Every night they shared the same bed, and their lovemaking became more intense and more satisfying. The word *love* was closer and closer to being said, at least by Charlie. He couldn't believe he had spent most of his life alone when being with someone now meant so much to him. He felt more certain than ever that fate has plans for us all, whether we're ready for what's coming or not.

The telephone call to Jake earlier turned out to be the most difficult call he had ever made, and afterwards, he wished that he hadn't even made it.

He began his conversation with his Hoosier buddy by telling him the story about his sister and niece, and he struggled as he attempted to bring Jake up to date with Susanna's life.

"I had a real hard time listening to that big city lawyer read Susanna's letter to me, Jake. Would you believe that she got pregnant in college and my folks sent her away to have her baby. That's the reason she moved to Denver. I just can't believe my parents would do that. Why do you think they sent her away?"

There was a long pause on the other end of the line. Then slowly but surely, Jake confessed.

"I don't know how to tell you this, Charlie, but I did know that Susanna was pregnant."

"How did you know? And why didn't you tell me? All these years you knew she had a baby and didn't tell me about it? I thought we were friends. You knew how much I thought about her and you didn't mention that to me? Some friend!"

Again there was an awkward moment as Jake seemed to be deciding how much to tell his best friend.

"Charlie, I swear I didn't know anymore than the fact that Susanna was expecting a kid. She told me she was going to Denver to live with an aunt, but I swear, that's all I know."

"How did you know she was pregnant?"

"Well ..."

"Come on, Jake. Who told you she was pregnant?"

"Susanna called me when she first got to school in Terre Haute and told me."

"Why would she have let you in on that information and not me?"

"Charlie, don't get mad."

"Why should I be mad, Jake? What's there for me to be mad about?" Charlie was half expecting what was coming next, but until the words were spoken, he didn't believe it.

"Please, Charlie. It was a long time ago, and we were at a going-away party. We were all drinking, and I took Susanna home afterwards, and, and, you know, you know what happened."

"You got my sister pregnant?"

"Susanna said it was me, but I don't know that for sure."

"Oh my God. My best friend gets my sister in trouble and doesn't even help her out. Nice guy, Jake. Were you ever going to tell me about it?"

There was only silence on the other end of the line as Charlie waited for an answer.

"Well, Jake. Were you going to tell me or not?"

"Charlie, I'm so sorry for what happened. I don't know what else to say, man. It was a long time ago. I'm truly sorry."

"Did you know that your daughter died? Do you even care? You know, Jake, I can hardly believe any of what I've learned in the last few days, especially what you're telling me now. One thing I know for sure, I don't ever want to talk to you again."

And with that, Charlie hung up the phone.

Charlie's hands were shaking, he was so upset with Jake, and he didn't even get to the part about asking him to sell his herd of cows. He knew they had to be sold, because with no one to look after the animals—and he surely didn't think Jake would be doing that anymore—they would all die before he could get home and get them to market. After calming down some, he knew he had to make one more call.

"Brenda, this is Charlie."

"Charlie Wintergreen? Are you back from Denver already?"

"No, I'm still there. Listen, Brenda, I wonder if you can get me the telephone number of LC. I need to call him and ask a favor of him."

"Sure, I'll get the number for you. Is everything okay?"

"Yes, everything is just fine. Just fine."

"Is there anything else I can do for you? Anything at all?"

"No, Brenda, I can't think of anything. Maybe I'll give you a call when I get back home."

"That would be great, Charlie. I would really like that. Here's the number you wanted."

Charlie's conversation with LC. was short—loud, but short—and the ninety-year-old farmer agreed to take the herd to market for Charlie.

"Don't worry about the cattle that have to be sold. This might not be the best time to be taking them to market, but I'll get you the best price I can and transport them to the sale barn in my grandson's truck," LC yelled into the mouthpiece.

Told to keep half of whatever price he got for the small herd as payment for selling them, LC said he wouldn't accept a penny for helping Charlie out but was sure missing his neighbor and hoped he would get home soon. "We talk about you every morning at the Comeback," he told Charlie. "We all hope you get back soon, especially Brenda. I think she's missing you more than anyone else."

"Thanks so much, LC. I'll call you as soon as I get home. Please tell everyone at the restaurant that I said hi. See you soon."

Charlie was so upset with what Jake told him that he could hardly think of anything else but his friend's confession. The one thing that might take his mind off the situation was Susanna's house, and he plunged headfirst into the remodeling job, hoping that if he kept busy enough, maybe the pain would go away. Charlie was beginning to believe that he couldn't trust anyone anymore.

"If I start tearing down the garage, do you want to pack up all of Susanna's belongings in the house?" They were standing together on the sidewalk out front of the rundown home in the Highlands. "That's one job I don't really want to do."

"Are we saving everything in the house or just her personal items?"

Ginny was dressed in jeans, a red flannel shirt, and moccasins as she spoke, a look that he had never seen on her before. Her hair was pulled back into a ponytail peeking out from the back of a Gutwein Seed baseball cap that Charlie had provided. She still appeared as if she could be on the cover of a fashion magazine, high dollar gorgeous. In her back pocket was a pair of gloves. The ersatz model turned construction worker was ready to pitch in but not get her hands dirty or fingernails broken.

They stood there outside the house, caught up in the moment, until Charlie realized that there was much work to be done and they needed to get started on it. He turned from Ginny to head to the garage as he yelled instructions over his shoulder.

"For now, let's just gather the photos and personal items and save them until we have a chance to sort through everything. Later, we can decide what to do with her clothing and jewelry and other stuff. Put the boxes of things you gather up on the back porch, along with the furniture we're going to save. We'll figure out what to do with it all later. I'm going to start on the garage, just to remove that eyesore, and then I can concentrate on the house afterward. After the garage is built, we'll take all of Susanna's belongings and put them inside the new building."

Ginny stopped him before he made it to the demolition job waiting for him in the back of the house. "Charlie, let's enjoy this moment. I don't know what's going to happen in the future, but I want you to know that I've never been happier in my life than I am right now. I'm so glad you decided to work on your sister's house. We can really turn this place into something nice, a home that she would be proud of. And we might even manage to make a few bucks off of it, if you decide to sell."

Charlie just nodded, but he had a smile on his face that spoke volumes about his feelings. Ginny sure did know the right things to say to make him feel good. He headed to the backyard, sledge hammer resting on his shoulder. Ginny made her way to the child's bedroom, a vision of dollar signs dancing in her head. It was time to get this project going!

chapter 9

LONG HOURS TURNED to days, and then weeks, and still there was much work to be done. It didn't take the neighbors long to recognize that something out of the ordinary was going on at the house, and one by one, they came by when they saw Charlie outside.

Most of the young couples who he met voiced only a "Hi, how are you?" as they walked past the house, all seemingly intrigued with the work going on there, and it was okay with him that they didn't stop. Some of those he met while they were passing by had small children in strollers, and they introduced themselves and told where they lived. He seldom remembered their names, thinking there would be plenty of time to talk with neighbors later. Everyone, it seemed, had a dog with them, and one young couple from the neighborhood walked five daily. More than once Charlie thought that Denver must be the most dog-friendly city in the country. Everyone seemed anxious to see the house when it was finished. He was kind of amazed at the friendliness of the people in Colorado, and he told anyone interested that he would make sure they saw the inside of the house when he was finished with it.

On one sunny morning, he had the opportunity to meet the only neighbor who seemed to know anything about his sister.

"Are you fixing up the old house to sell or are you going to live here?" the attractive blonde asked as she stopped him in front of the house.

Robin was a pediatric nurse who had lived across the street from Susanna for years and who had been watching anxiously for an opportunity to talk to whoever it was working on her deceased neighbor's house. When she saw Charlie carrying out a load of trash to the dumpster, she seized the moment and crossed to his side of the street.

Her hair was pulled back in a ponytail, and she was dressed in jeans, a T-shirt, and flip-flops, looking to Charlie like she was more ready for summer than the time of year they were currently experiencing. Her casual appearance the norm in the neighborhood, though. She was cute, with bright blue eyes that sparkled like the Kashmir sapphire ring that his mother wore on special occasions, and her looks weren't lost on him.

"Don't know for sure," he replied, wondering who it was that was asking. "Right now my interest is in fixing up my sister's house. When I'm finished, I'll decide what I'm going to do with it."

"You're Susanna's brother?" She had an incredulous look on her face as she asked the question, as if she really didn't believe Charlie.

"I'm sorry," Charlie said as he reached his hand out to her. "I should have introduced myself. My name is Charlie Wintergreen, and yes, ma'am, I was her only sibling."

"I didn't know there was a brother, or any relative for that matter," Robin replied as she gently took his hand in hers. "Did you ever visit?"

He hesitated before answering, wondering just how much he should share with a stranger.

"No. Can't say that I ever did," he answered, glancing at the ground as he spoke, more than a little ashamed at the thought of not even knowing that his sister had lived in Denver. "And to tell you the truth, I feel awful about that. My sister and I were real close when we were kids, but after she left for college, I never saw her again. I didn't even know that she lived here until she died and a lawyer got in touch with me."

"What did you say your name was?" he finally asked after a few moments of awkward silence.

"I'm Robin Richey. I live across the street, and I knew your sister quite well. I took care of all her funeral arrangements when she died and made sure she had a proper burial." She was standing close enough to Charlie that she saw the grimace on his face as she spoke and knew that she had brought up a subject that he knew nothing about.

"Oh my gosh! To think that someone who wasn't even family had to take care of her final expenses really makes me feel terrible. I thank you for that, Robin. If I had known about her death sooner, I would have seen to the arrangements myself. Can I repay you for your kindness?"

The nurse looked at her friend's brother skeptically, probably wondering why someone who hadn't ever visited would even care if Susanna had been treated right at the end of her life or not.

"No, I don't think so. I'm glad I was able to help a friend out."

"Well then, I thank you very much for your kindness, and if there is anything I can ever do for you, I hope you won't hesitate to ask."

Charlie knew that if anyone would know anything about his sister, it would be Robin, and she probably held a wealth of information about Susanna that she might be willing to share with him.

"Listen, Robin. You and I probably have a lot to talk about, as I'd sure like to find out as much about Susanna's life here as I can. Is it possible you could stop by later this evening and maybe we can have a cup of coffee and talk about her life here in the neighborhood?"

She looked at him curiously, obviously thinking about her response before finally answering him.

"I'll be over around seven."

"Great. I look forward to our conversation then."

Robin crossed the street to her house, occasionally looking over her shoulder at the man she just met, most likely wondering just what kind of family Susanna had.

With her departure, Charlie turned his attention back to the task at hand. There was much to be done, but he was enjoying the challenge of fixing up the old place. His one-month lease on the condo had expired, and despite Ginny's insistence that he move into her unit, Charlie decided to live in his sister's house while he was working on it as he now realized how much effort it would take to finish the project. He wanted to be working at sunup, he told her, and the only way to do that was to sleep in the house. She declined to join him because they would be sleeping in Susanna's bed and she wasn't comfortable with the thought of doing that.

Robin arrived that evening, dressed much differently than earlier, and she had an aroma about her as if she just stepped out of a bubble bath. To Charlie, her appearance made her look like she was going to be dining out at a nice restaurant. It wasn't that she didn't appear attractive earlier, but a change of clothes and hair done differently gave her a fresh look, and he was quick to notice the difference. She brought a chocolate cake she made for the occasion, and Charlie put on a pot of coffee as soon as she showed up at the front door.

After exchanging pleasantries and dining on the freshly baked dessert, he asked Robin what she could tell him about his sister. He was enjoying his conversation with her, and he wasn't in any hurry for her to leave. She didn't seem to want to leave either.

"I moved across the street after Susanna's daughter died," Robin began. "So I didn't know the little girl at all, but I did get to know your sister, and over the years we became friends. She didn't talk about her daughter very often, and eventually, she hardly mentioned her at all."

"Did she ever talk about her relatives?"

"She told me she was from a small town in Indiana and that her family were farmers, but that's about all she ever said."

"I guess I don't blame her for that," Charlie said. "After the way she was treated by everyone, why would she want people to know anything about us?

"I don't even know how she died. Do you?"

"I think officially the doctor who came to the house said she in all probability had a heart attack, but I think she just died of a broken heart. Your sister was the loneliest person I ever met in my life. Everyday was a struggle for her."

"Did she work? How did she support herself?"

"Well, she did have a job at the library over by the park, but I don't think it paid very much," Robin replied. "I don't think she had much in her life, but she acted like she didn't need very much. She was pretty content with the little bit that life had given her."

She shifted uneasily in her chair as she said, "You do know that she was an alcoholic, don't you?"

Charlie looked straight at Robin but didn't seem to be too taken aback by her comment. "I really don't know anything about my sister. I sure didn't know that she drank like that. She never drank when she was at home."

Charlie realized now that the odor he smelled when he first entered Susanna's house was the smell of booze.

"She wasn't one of those obnoxious drunks that come to some people's minds when they hear the word *alcoholic*. But I believe she drank every night and drank until she fell asleep. At least she drank the entire time I knew her. I guess that was her way of shutting out all the badness that seemed to surround her. Your sister blamed herself for the death of her daughter, no matter what the official report said."

Charlie noticed that Robin's cup was empty and brought the coffee pot back to fill it.

"No, thank you, Charlie. If I drink any more coffee, I won't be able to sleep tonight. I have to work in the morning."

"Do you know what caused Darla's death?" Charlie asked as he refilled his coffee cup. "Because in the letter she left for me, she said that her daughter had died after being sick for a while."

"All I know is what she shared with me, and like I said, after a while, she stopped talking about her entirely."

"Go on."

"She told me the child had fallen off a swing in the backyard and hit her head. Susanna was napping in the house at the time, probably full of the gin she drank, and didn't hear her scream for help. By the time someone called an ambulance and got her to a hospital, she had suffered so much brain damage that she couldn't be helped.

"Your sister never did forgive herself for that, even though the initial fall probably caused most of the damage and not the delay in getting her to a doctor.

"The child lived for some time after the fall, but she was never normal again. Poor little thing. And your sister was probably never the same again either."

Charlie was having a hard time absorbing everything that Robin was telling him; his mind kept flashing back to the photo of Darla that he saw on the wall when he entered his sister's house, and he was more than a little upset with himself because he wasn't around to help either Susanna or her daughter during their time of need.

"I can't imagine what Susanna went through. I'm just sorry I didn't know about her situation while she was still alive. I might have been able to help her."

"Yes, I suppose you or some other relative could have helped her. It probably would have changed the course of the rest of her life. She might even still be alive today if only someone would have just helped her some."

When Robin left that evening, Charlie decided that he still didn't know much about his sister, but he was glad he met Robin so that some of the pieces of the puzzle came together for him. He told Robin that if she ever remembered anything else that might be useful, to let him know. He was kind of hoping she would remember things daily.

There was a hesitancy as she left that night, on both their parts, and Robin walked slowly back to her house across the street, telling Charlie that maybe they could get together again sometime.

"I'd like that," Charlie replied, "I really would." He watched her until she climbed the front stairs to her home, turned, and waved good-bye to him, and then closed the front door behind her.

He was thinking that Robin was really a nice person and he would have liked to have met her under different circumstances.

Charlie had never been depressed about anything in his life, even after both his parents passed away. No matter how many curves life threw at him, he was always able to suck it up and go on living as if he wasn't affected by the events.

But the last few weeks had been much more difficult than anything he had ever been confronted with before, and he walked around as if a cloud of doom hung over his head. The subcontractors working around him would probably say that he wasn't much fun to be around anymore. He immersed himself in his work, hoping that by staying busy, somehow the dark cloud hovering overhead would disappear. Thoughts of Darla swirled in his head as he tried to envision how she must have looked and acted. He wondered if she had the same playful spirit as her mother and knew that he would have enjoyed being with her and loving her. He spent many waking hours wishing that things had turned out differently for the little girl and for her mother.

The nice weather continued, and the days were long and pleasant, encouraging the man to work even longer hours than in the beginning, and on one particular day, he finally laid down his tools around midnight, turned off the country music station he had grown to like, and undressed. He was exhausted and even deferred a shower until the morning. Bed would feel good this evening. Ginny had left earlier after bringing Chinese carryout for dinner, which he ate reluctantly, calling it a meal similar to one that he would feed his cattle, but they finished everything she brought and even had a good laugh reading the predictions inside the fortune cookies.

He had slept soundly, for what seemed like hours, when he was awakened by a feeling that someone was in the room with him. There was no certainty to the cause of his awakening, no noise, no bright light, not even a nightmare; it was more a feeling than anything else. He lay in bed, shade pulled, lights out, doors locked, and listened.

There was no sound outside of the normal creaking and groaning noises that the old house made every night.

He felt like someone was intruding into the room, though. He sensed it more than saw it. Half sitting up in bed, he looked around and didn't see anything out of the ordinary or hear anything moving. But someone or something had gone bump in the night, causing him to awaken. Goose bumps ran up and down his arms as he thought about the possibility of an intruder, and he instinctively reached for the can that should have been in his back pocket when he remembered he wasn't wearing pants.

Charlie hadn't given much thought to the possibility of someone breaking in; he never even locked his house back home in Indiana and was certain, even now, a thousand miles away from home, it still wasn't locked. But this was a big city he was in, and if anyone had been watching the house, they probably had seen the work going on inside and wondered if there could be expensive tools inside

He got up then and walked around the house in the dark, checking doors and windows to make sure they were locked. They were. Looking outside, the streets and sidewalks were clear of the presence of trouble and his rental car was sitting where he had parked it earlier. He felt better about that and went back to bed and eventually to sleep but was restless, his eyes darting opening at every noise, until he finally arose in the morning, not feeling rested at all.

When he did get up, he couldn't help but wonder what caused him to awaken in the middle of the night. He thought he might have had indigestion from the rice, noodles, and other cattle feed that he and Ginny ate before he went to bed. Either that or he felt his imagination was working overtime and he just dreamed the entire thing. Whatever it was, Charlie began to realize how many hours he had been working at the house and decided that he needed a break for a few days. He would ask Ginny to take him to Winter Park or someplace else in the mountains that weekend. Ginny had been telling Charlie about the ski resorts in the mountains, and it was a perfect opportunity to see them in person.

He put on a pot of coffee, turned on the radio, and headed for the shower.

Thoughts of the day's work filled his mind as he dressed afterward and sipped on the first cup of coffee of the day. Country music legend Alan Jackson was singing a love song on the radio and made him think of Ginny and the way he had been treating her lately.

Charlie had been in a funk and knew that he had to get on with his life in order to feel better. He knew that he was already doing all that he could to make things right in Susanna's memory and needed to stop walking around like he was mad at the world. A trip to the mountains would certainly help clear his head, and after deciding that was what he wanted to do that weekend, went back to work on the house.

Charlie had pulled up all the carpet in the house except in Darla's room. That would be his first task of the day. He thought he could get that finished before Ginny arrived, and then she could help carry the carpet out to the roll-off in front of the house.

As he entered his niece's room, Charlie turned on the overhead light and stopped dead in his tracks. He stood there, as if in a trance, staring in amazement at what he was seeing. Everything that had been removed from the room previously had been returned: the bed in the corner, pictures on the walls, clothes in the closet—everything. A chill ran down his spine as he surveyed the scene in front of him.

Charlie couldn't believe what he was seeing. He knew everything had been taken out of the bedroom weeks ago, and he had looked in the girl's room many times since then. Each time the room had been empty.

His first instinct was to turn around and leave, but the more he thought about it, the more he was inclined to believe that there had to be a logical explanation for what had happened, and so he entered the room to get a better look at what was there.

Items weren't just returned, he discovered. They were in the exact place they had been in when he first saw Darla's room. He ran his hands over furniture and pictures to ensure the presence of them and prove, if only to himself, that they weren't imaginary. He left the room and quickly walked out to the new garage, where they had temporarily stored the items after they were removed from the bedroom, hoping that maybe he was still half-asleep and merely seeing things in the room that didn't exist. The garage still had many displaced items in it, but all of his niece's belongings were gone.

When Ginny arrived and was shown the bedroom, she was as puzzled as Charlie was but didn't act as if was a big deal, so they once again took everything out of the room and placed the items where they had been previously.

"Someone is pulling a joke on us," Ginny said, and they both laughed an uneasy kind of laugh, like neither one of them believed what she suggested but wanted the other to think they did.

"I can't explain what happened here either, Charlie. I think we both need a break from this house for a while."

"I think you're right, Ginny. I know I definitely need a break."

Afterward, they pulled up the carpet and threw it in the large container outside, now almost full with discards from the house. The hardwood floors in the bedroom were in the best shape of any they'd seen so far and gave them a hint of how beautiful the flooring would look when refinished.

That weekend they drove to Winter Park in the high country to get away from the work at the house, and Charlie fell in love with the area.

The tall pine trees seemed to reach to the sky as the highway wound its way around and over scenery that he had never seen before.

"My God, Ginny, this part of the state is so beautiful," he repeated after every turn in the road, "just beautiful." Tall peaks surrounded them, mountains taller than anything he had seen so far, and the smell of junipers filled the crisp, cool air. It was a good smell, one that reminded of him of Christmas when he was a boy on the farm.

"Now this is what I thought Colorado was going to be like—stunning scenery, cool temperatures, and a feeling that you're in a place that probably hasn't changed that much over the years. It is picture-postcard perfect!"

Ginny just smiled as he spoke, excited over Charlie's enthusiasm.

"It is beautiful, isn't it? You should see the area during the height of the ski season. It's even better."

Despite the fact that skiing had ended a few weeks earlier, there was still snow in places, and the ski runs were quite visible. He found the area to be charming, even without tons of white stuff on the ground.

"Is there anything to do here when it's not winter, or is skiing all there is?"

"If a person likes the outdoors, he would love the ski resort areas year round, as there are hiking and biking trails, and a new development here is building beautiful ski-in, ski-out homes and a professional golf course. I think you would really enjoy living here."

"How about things to do for kids?" he asked. 'What would they do here?"

"You're kidding me, right? Children in Colorado ski. They have classes for beginners that start at age three. And as I said earlier, people who live around here are outdoor types who would ride their bikes or take hikes on trails or do just about anything that kids would do anywhere."

"I noticed some cattle grazing in the meadows as we were driving up here. Are there a lot of cattle ranchers around this area?"

"Now you're asking me questions that I can't answer. I saw the animals on the way here, also, but I don't know the difference between a cow and a steer and don't have a clue about anything related to ranching or farming."

Unfazed by her answer, Charlie continued looking out the window at the scenery, enjoying the spectacular views. "Now, I could live here," he told her, "even if I don't ski. I'd like to come back again sometime," he said. Ginny promised they would.

chapter 10

MONDAY CAME MUCH too quickly, and soon it was back to work on the project in the Highlands. The weekend trip to the mountain ski resort area was so restful that it was hard to get back into the groove of hard work again, but the remodeling job wouldn't be completed by itself, and so paint brushes found their way into cans of color, and the day was spent applying that to waiting walls.

Charlie was his old self again, working as hard as he had in the beginning of the project while listening to his favorite radio station. He even bought lunch for the electrician and plumber who were working on the house with him. Laughter and good-natured banter filled the empty house once more.

Before retiring that night, thoughts of time spent in the mountains filled his mind, and he wondered again what it was about the high country that seemed to call to him. But call it did, and he couldn't wait to return and spend more time there. He didn't think he would ever learn how to ski, but he just liked the idea of being in the higher elevations where the air was clean and the hustle and bustle of the city was far away.

He made sure all of the doors and windows in the house were locked before turning in for the night. Satisfied that no one was going to enter without great effort, Charlie took one last look into Darla's bedroom, found it to be as empty as he hoped it would be, and fell asleep the moment his head hit the pillow. He dreamed of his little niece taking skiing lessons with visions of high mountain peaks in the background.

Sometime before morning, he woke out of a sound sleep and lay quietly listening for whatever it was that caused him to awaken. This time it was more than a feeling that someone was in the room with him. He actually felt something touch him and wake him, much like his mother did when he was still a boy and there were chores to do before school. She would enter his room and merely touch him on his arm or shoulder, not even saying his name. She knew that would be enough to wake him. It felt like that.

When he opened his eyes, he was surprised that he didn't see anyone or hear anything. He almost uttered, "I'm awake, Mother." Then he realized he wasn't at home and there would be no school to attend this day. Nothing seemed to be out of the ordinary. His eyes had become somewhat accustomed to the darkness of night, and he could see that there wasn't anyone in the room with him. He rose from bed and walked across the hallway to Darla's room and turned on the light, his heart racing with the anxiety of not knowing what to expect. Once again, all of the furniture was back in the room, including the carpet, which had been ripped out and thrown away.

"Oh, my God!" Charlie said in disbelief at the sight in front of him. "Someone is either playing a terrible trick on me or there is something, what's it called, paranormal, going on in this room. I'm hoping someone is just having some fun at my expense. If I didn't know better, I'd swear someone or something is trying to scare us out of this house."

He was too upset to go back to bed, so he dressed, left the house in a hurry, and drove to Ginny's place. He didn't want to stay in the house by himself, so he acted as if he wanted her input into what they should be working on that week and then spent the rest of the night worrying about all the craziness happening at Susanna's house.

In the morning, they returned to the house where unexplained things were occurring, went inside, and looked in the child's room. It still contained all the objects that were originally in the room the first day they saw it.

"I don't know what is going on, Charlie, but I'm getting a little concerned. You don't think the house is haunted, do you?"

"I'll be honest with you. I don't have a clue as to what is causing this to happen, but I'm sure going to find out."

"I want you to stay here with me tonight, okay? Maybe if the two of us are here, one of us can sleep while the other stays awake, and we'll see whoever or whatever it is that's moving this furniture back to the room. We can remove everything one more time and see if it somehow finds its way back in again."

"Are you out of your mind? I'm not ever spending a night in this house until we find out what's causing the furniture to mysteriously reappear in that room. Never, Charlie. Do you hear me? Never!"

"Okay, okay, calm down. I'll stay by myself. Now help me move the furniture."

She thought about if for a minute and then said, "Let's leave things the way they are. Maybe someone or something doesn't want that room empty. I think we ought to leave it alone, maybe even lock it up until we decide what we're going to do with the house."

He agreed to try that solution but still wanted her to stay with him that evening. She was pretty adamant about not being there at night, though, and he didn't want to upset her any more than she already was, so he didn't carry the conversation any further. He didn't want to tell her he was a little apprehensive about staying there by himself.

Not much was accomplished that day as his thoughts never strayed far from the situation in the bedroom. Ginny left at dark, telling him to be careful and leaving him her cell phone so he could phone her or call for help if he needed to.

"Are you sure you want to do this? Why don't you stay at my place tonight?"

"No, I'll be all right," he insisted. "I want to find out what is going on here, and I can't do that if I'm not here."

Ginny left him then, and as she was driving home, she couldn't help but wonder if she hadn't gotten herself into a bad situation with the house remodeling job. The project had been going all right until recently, and she could tell that Charlie was really taking a liking to her. She was doing all she could to make him fall in love with her. All she had to do was get past the nonsense that was going on in

Darla's bedroom and it would be smooth sailing for the rest of the renovation. Then she was certain she could talk Charlie into marrying her or at the least sharing some of the money that he'd make off the sale of the house. Everything was going according to plan except for this one little setback, and she was certain she could overcome that.

Charlie checked the house before going to bed; everything seemed to be secured, and he decided to leave the light on in Darla's room. Sleep didn't come easily, and he tossed and turned for hours, waiting for something to happen, but eventually he fell into a fitful slumber, expecting to be awakened before the sun rose. He wasn't.

Nothing happened the following evening either, or the one after that. Eventually, he went back to his original routine and gave the cell phone back to Ginny, saying that he didn't think he would need it. Ginny wasn't so convinced but realized she wasn't going to change Charlie's mind.

And then one night, in the early morning hours before it was time to arise, he felt the same presence near him that he had sensed before and awoke to a sight that was unexplainable and absolutely frightening. Someone was in the room with him, and for the first time, he saw who it was. Despite the darkness of the room, there was a light. Not the kind one would expect to see coming from an electric bulb, and it didn't fill the room with brightness. It was more like the arrival of dawn when you've been sound asleep and your eyes begin to open to the beginning of a new day coming through the blinds of a bedroom window.

What he saw was an outline of a person hovering close to the bed, feet not touching the floor, moving in an unhurried motion towards him. At first he couldn't tell if it was a man or woman, adult or child.

There was an aura surrounding the shape like a back-lit cloud, more surreal than real, and it prevented him from seeing anything more than a dark image. As it neared, the entire area, not more than three or four feet high and wide, appeared almost transparent, like a jelly fish swimming in the ocean, a mere wisp of something or someone, like if you reached out to touch it, your hand would go through to the other side.

And then he realized that it was a child, a little girl, maybe five or six years old, that had been slowly moving towards him. She had long, red, curly hair and wore a floral print dress that hung to her ankles. She looked exactly like the child in the photograph he saw the first day they entered the house. Her right hand was outstretched, like she was trying to touch him. Fear was not something Charlie had to deal with very often in his life, but at this moment, nothing else could describe what he was feeling. His eyes never left hers as he sat up in bed and the little girl neared him. He was wet with perspiration, yet cold, like he was coming down with some kind of illness. The room was perfectly still.

"What do you want?" he asked.

No response.

"Who are you?"

Again, there was no answer, only a bewildered look as the child moved, first closer to him as if she might touch him, then away as if she feared him. Then she was gone.

He shook his head. Maybe it was just a dream, he thought, but if it wasn't that, what was it? A ghost? He really didn't believe in such things, yet what else could it have been? He waited to see if the vision might return, not certain what he would do if it did. The room was as empty now as it was when he had retired for the night. He got out of bed, both him and the sheets damp from his nervous perspiration, and quietly tiptoed into the other bedroom, not knowing what to expect when he got there. The light in the child's room was still on, but the room itself was empty of anything abnormal. Everything seemed to be in place, and he was turning to leave when he noticed the black and white framed photo of him and Susanna taken in front of their farmhouse in Indiana was missing. He knew it had been on the dresser earlier, the same place it always was. Who could have moved that, he wondered, and why?

Charlie was certain now he wasn't dreaming. No one else had been in the house that night, but someone or something had been in the room to remove the photo. But who was it and what did they want? Charlie wondered if someone was trying to warn him of danger. Or were they trying to hurt him? As scared as he was when it was happening, he knew he couldn't leave until he found out the meaning of all the strange things occurring there.

When Ginny arrived in the morning, Charlie told her what happened during the night, including seeing the apparition in his room.

"I don't know what it was, Ginny," he said. "But it sure looked like my niece. If it was her, what does she want? And why is her ghost hanging around the house? Maybe she doesn't want me or anyone else disturbing her things."

The color had drained out of Charlie's face as he told the story, like he really had seen a ghost, and Ginny could tell that he was truly upset about the incident. So was she.

"Charlie, you're really starting to scare the hell out of me. I think you are seeing things, I really do, and you need to stop sleeping in this house at night. I want you to promise me that you'll stay at my place at nighttime from now on. Please, Charlie. You're getting awfully scary talking about ghosts and furniture moving around on its own and stuff."

"I can't do that, Ginny. Something is going on in this house, and I have to find out what it is. That little girl who appeared to me last night reached out to me like she was trying to touch me or tell me something. I don't think she was trying to hurt me. I've got to find out what's going on here."

Ginny made it quite clear that she would never step foot inside the house again. She left him standing on the front porch, telling him he was frigging crazy for remaining there.

"I'm sorry, Charlie, but I can't continue helping you. This whole thing is way too crazy for me. I don't know if it is you or the house or both, but I can't help you here anymore. I'm sorry. Call me sometime when all the spooks have stopped visiting you."

No matter how much arguing he did, there was no convincing her otherwise, and he was finally left to wonder if the relationship that he had been so carefully cultivating might be coming to an end.

This can't be happening to me, Ginny thought as she pulled away from the house in the Highlands. *I've worked too hard for too long to see it all unravel now. What the heck is wrong with Charlie? Could he have possibly seen what he says he has? I doubt it. Maybe he's caught on to my gig and is just trying to get rid of me.*

chapter 11

FROM THAT DAY on, Charlie went to bed each evening, hoping the vision would reappear, but it didn't. Work continued on the project, despite the duress of believing that someone or something inhabited the house, and eventually all the painting was completed in every room but Darla's. He was as nervous as the proverbial whore in church the entire time, and the slightest unexpected sound would cause him to flinch and cower as if an incoming round in combat was falling near him. He wasn't afraid of what he had seen that night, but was the occurrence a warning of something more sinister? He didn't know the answer, and because he wasn't certain what else might take place in the house during the middle of the night, he remained constantly on edge. His intake of tobacco increased, as did the amount of antacid tablets consumed.

Darla's bedroom was avoided at all costs, but sooner or later the job would have to be finished if the house was going to be sold. Peeking in the room each time he walked by, he had an expectation that something weird might happen, but nothing ever did, and he was both glad and saddened by that. Saddened because he wanted to see whatever it was that was in his room that night, but not at the expense of getting scared out of his jockey shorts.

When the outside of the one-and-a-half-story structure had been completed, the finished house appeared much the same as it probably did when new. The farmer-turned-house-remodeler was proud of his work but was getting antsy for the project to end. He wondered if he should tell the realtor about the mystery in the child's bedroom, but that thought didn't linger very long. No one would believe him anyway. There was no certainty concerning leaving Colorado for home. The decision to leave would all depend on Ginny, and he hadn't seen or heard from her in weeks. If ever there was a time in his life when he needed someone to lean on and take comfort in, it was now, but once again, he was alone.

Repeated calls to her cell phone went unanswered no matter what time of day or night he called. For whatever reason, Ginny was no longer a part of his life, and he was having a hard time dealing with that state of affairs. She had never told him that she loved him, but he wondered why she couldn't come around once in a while to see how he was doing. What was it she had proclaimed the day they began work on the remodeling job? "I've never been happier in my life than I am this day."

Charlie was beginning to believe that what Ginny expressed to him that day was a feeling that only lasted while everything was going all right in her life. He thought they had something between them that would last a lifetime. All her absence was doing was reinforcing how little Charlie knew about women. Eventually he came to the decision that it was probably a good thing that the work on the house was about finished. He would soon be going back home and to the only life he'd ever known: farming.

Charlie went to bed that evening deep in thought over his life back East. He wasn't sorry that he traveled to the western city. He had known a woman's love while there, and despite not wanting it to ever end, he was glad that he had met someone who ended up putting a deep ache in his heart. His relationship with her proved, if nothing else, that he was capable of loving another, and more important, of being loved. He wouldn't ever again believe that he couldn't find a woman to love. There was a definite sorrow to his being after learning about the tragedy that was Susanna's life, but he would no longer have to wonder about what had happened to her. It was still hard for him to believe that his parents had treated his sister and her baby the way they did, and he didn't think he could ever forgive them for that.

Then there was Darla. He wished that she was still alive for him to love, and he was convinced that's who paid him a visit in his room that night. But what did she want? He didn't really believe in ghosts but knew there are a lot of unexplained things that happen in life that leave people scratching their heads in disbelief, and this might be one of them. He believed that he saw something that night— exactly what it was, he wasn't certain.

Ever since he first saw the vision of the child, thoughts of her were never far away. Did her spirit inhabit the house that she had lived in during her short time on earth? If so, why? Was it because she died while living there? Or was there some kind of connection between the child and him? He fell asleep dreaming about his niece and woke up hours later with the spirit of her in his room again. It was as if the first time was being replayed in his mind.

The little girl appeared in a cloud of backlit light, barely visible, like a dream being watched through the eyes of someone else, moving slowly toward the bed.

He sat up when he sensed there was someone in the room with him and knew instantly who it was.

"Darla? Are you Darla?" he asked while looking through half-opened eyes.

This time there wasn't any fear in his voice as he spoke. He knew who was in the room with him. There wasn't a reply as the apparition slowly moved closer to him, drifting like a big, fluffy cloud overhead on a blue sky summer day. There was something in her hand, and at first, he couldn't make out what it was. As she neared, he could see that it was the photo of him and Susanna that had been on her dresser. She was holding it in one hand and pointing to it with the other while her face had a quizzical look about it. He realized that the little girl in front of him was wondering if that was him in the picture.

"Yes. I'm Uncle Charlie. Please tell me, are you Darla?"

She smiled then, and as she reached out to him, he felt something brush across his cheek like an early spring wind. The movement took his breath away, not because of the force of it but because of the tenderness and the idea of what it was that was happening to him.

He was being caressed by the ghost of his niece as if she was glad that he was in her house and happy to meet an uncle she had only heard about. Tears welled up in his eyes and a feeling of total elation filled his heart.

Charlie felt like the whole thing was a dream, or maybe he was just imagining that Darla's presence was with him now. Real or not, he found himself in the presence of something. What that was, he wasn't certain.

He knelt down on the floor then and put his arms out to see what the child would do, and she understood and moved into them.

He could feel her spirit, it was all around him. The child was caressing him, consoling him, loving him as he tried to engulf her in his arms.

In his mind, he thought he could hear her laughing; it was the kind of laugh that instantly turns an adult into a child himself, and he wanted to laugh with her.

Then he heard the words, *Love the children. Love the children,* and didn't know who said them or if they were spoken at all. He looked at the child. She was smiling at him and nodded an assent, as if acknowledging that she had spoken the words.

"Who?" he asked. "Who do I love? Which children?"

Love the children was the reply he heard, and he was certain that the words were coming from the little girl standing in front of him. But what did they mean?

She was moving now, with her hand outstretched behind her as if she wanted him to follow.

He did.

Across the hallway and into the child's bedroom they went, him two steps behind her. When they reached the closet, the door opened, and she stood in the closet and pointed to the ceiling. There was a trap door to the attic, a door Charlie never paid much attention to previously.

"You want me to see something in the attic?" he asked. "What's up there?" Again, she only pointed above, but he thought he heard someone talking. *Do you know about my mommy? My mommy cries every time she talks about Grandma. Why does my mommy cry so much?*

He shuddered at the thoughts going through his mind and left hurriedly to retrieve a step ladder from a part of the house where he had been painting. In the few moments he was away, the spirit that led him to the closet had disappeared and he was beginning to wonder if he might have been dreaming the whole thing. As crazy as it sounded, he would have felt safer if the spirit that led him to the attic door was still by his side. He ascended the steps anyway, not knowing what he might be getting into, and with some difficulty, he raised the cover off the opening and peered into the darkness. There was no light bulb. It was pitch black and cold, like he had entered a cave where any wild thing might be lurking, and he wondered what it was that might be hidden in the dark, cavernous reaches of the attic. He would need a flashlight.

Retrieving a light from his tool chest, he again climbed the six-foot step ladder and poked his head into the obscurity above, the flashlight his only weapon against the unknown awaiting him. The light from the flashlight showed fuzzy dirt floating through the air from disturbing the years-old dust, and a top story of the house that didn't contain much of anything. There were a few old orange crates, looking naked and useless, some wooden boards lying on top of the rafters, and a rather large number of empty gin bottles, dusty necks poking out from underneath loose insulation. The light didn't reveal much of anything else. He was ready to stop looking further until the light of day when he spotted a rather large cardboard box in the corner, barely visible from behind the fireplace chimney.

Carrying the box down the steps proved to be difficult as the cardboard container was heavy and awkward. When it was finally opened, years of accumulating dust flew off the top of the box, filling the room with enough pollutants to make him sneeze repeatedly. Inside, the box was filled with memorabilia from Darla's childhood, and he sat cross-legged on the floor, going through what turned out to be a treasure trove of information. Baby rattles, small stuffed animals, finger paintings, and other mementos that would be meaningless to anyone else but family were neatly stacked inside the cardboard container. One unframed photograph was of his sister and niece, and he could see the resemblance between the two, especially the red hair they both shared. Digging a little deeper, he found stacks of letters from Charlie's mother to Susanna.

At first he didn't want to read what was in them, but curiosity finally got the best of him and he pulled out the letters from the depths of the box and looked at the dates on the envelopes before opening them.

Charlie remembered what the child asked: "Why does my mommy cry when she talks about Grandma?" He wondered if he might discover why Susanna cried when talking about their mother, and if Darla already knew the answer.

Paging through the stack of time-worn envelopes, he found what was probably the first one sent to Susanna, or at least the first one saved. The date corresponded with about the time that she disappeared. He couldn't believe that his mother had written his sister for years and didn't tell him, or perhaps anyone else, about her whereabouts. He opened up the unsealed envelope and read what his mother had written.

Susanna, I know this must be very difficult for you. It certainly is for your father and me. But Aunt Bonnie has agreed to take you in until the baby is born and given away. Afterward, you can come back home. Folks will think you have just stayed at school and won't know that you were pregnant.

I think it is best for all concerned that you don't call home.

Enclosed is an airplane ticket to Denver and enough money to get you settled once you arrive there. I'll send more later.

Love, Mother.

Other letters were more revealing, and it soon became apparent that once the unmarried daughter decided to keep the baby, her parents weren't happy with that decision at all, and she was told so repeatedly in the letters. She was also warned not to call home, as her father wanted nothing to do with her or the baby, and he would take his anger out on her mother if she did call. And then he found the one letter that seemed to sum up the situation best for him. It was the skeleton in the closet that most families have and are usually ashamed to talk about until forced to do so. It was all news to him and quite disturbing.

Susanna, I'm going to tell you something that I've never told anyone else. Your father knows, but we haven't spoken of this in years. I was born out of wedlock. My mother wasn't married when she became pregnant with me. Back in those days, women who made that mistake in their lives were treated like they had a deadly disease, and my mother was shamed out of the small town she lived in by what happened to her. She never married, although she lied about that many times, telling me and everyone else who asked that my father had been killed in an accident before I was born. I was both shocked and mad when I heard the truth, but not too shocked, because at the time she told me, I was pregnant with you and, like my mother before me, not married.

Fortunately, even though he wasn't very happy about the situation, your father was a good enough man to marry me and raise you like you belonged to him. I don't believe anyone in town knows the story about either me or my mother, as I met your father soon after I learned I was expecting, and we didn't tell anyone about my situation.

I'm just so sorry that you have to learn about all this in a letter from me. I should have told you about everything long ago, but I was too embarrassed to do so. I'm not proud of my mistakes, but just as you discovered, life happens.

When your father learned of your decision to keep the baby, he was livid and told me that there would be no more bastards in the Wintergreen family. He said he was tired of living with loose women and there wouldn't ever be another one in his life.

I've pleaded with him many times, asking him, "Who's going to love the child? She'll have no one to love her." He doesn't care. He said, "Let someone else love the children of whores."

Charlie put the letter down then and tried to imagine what Susanna must have been thinking after reading the letter from their mother.

First, Susanna learned about her mother getting pregnant with her when she wasn't married; then her father called her a whore and said let someone else love her child. That would have been enough to make a saint want to get drunk and stay that way.

He picked up the letter again.

The words spoken by the child now made more sense: *Love the children.*

Could it be that's what Darla was trying to tell me? Charlie wondered. *Was she just repeating what she heard from that letter? Or was she asking me to somehow do what our parents refused to do: love her.* But how could he possibly do that now that she was gone?

Darla led him to the box of letters in the attic. He probably wouldn't have discovered the letters if not for someone or something leading him to the attic opening.

He still couldn't believe what had been happening, and more than anything, he wanted to share that with the one person he loved. He tried for hours to get in touch with her, to no avail. Even in the middle of the night, Ginny wouldn't take his calls.

During the week it took to complete the work on the house, he spoke with Robin again, but never saw his niece or girlfriend. He enjoyed the time he spent with his neighbor, and she seemed to be warming up to him. At least she laughed more these days and acted more comfortable around him. With the absence of Ginny, his new friend was filling the void that was now in his life. After being told what was discovered in the attic, Robin claimed she didn't know anything about Susanna receiving mail from home.

"She didn't share that kind of information with me," she told him. "And I doubt if I would have told anyone about that, either, if that were me in that situation."

Charlie didn't mention seeing the vision because he didn't think she would believe him. He enjoyed his con-

versation with Robin, though, and found her to be someone who loved being around and taking care of children.

On his last trip to Ginny's condo, Charlie discovered
that she had moved out and had not left a forwarding address. He was pretty upset about that news, and at first
didn't want to believe it.

Charlie couldn't imagine why Ginny would just leave
him like that. He actually thought that they might spend
the rest of their lives together. Now she was gone. His parents were dead, his sister as well, and the only child of his
sister was dead, too. And the one woman who lately had
meant the most to him had left him. What was fate doing
to him, he wondered. What damn direction was he supposed to go in now?

While at the condo, he saw and spoke with Bill, the
maintenance man in the building. Bill knew everyone and
everything going on in the complex. When Charlie asked
him about Ginny, he was told that the rumor was that she
had met some widower one night while swimming in the
pool, and they had become pretty good friends. When the
man decided to move to San Francisco to be close to his
adult children, she went with him.

"You do know that woman was just chasing money,
don't you?" Bill asked. "She didn't have a nickel to her name
and tried to hustle money from every man she came in contact with. If you don't mind me asking, I hope you didn't
give her a credit card or bank account number, did you?"

"She told me her husband had left her lots of money."

"Well, I don't think that was the truth. To be honest
with you, all of us who work here were pretty worried that
she might take you to the cleaners if you let her get too

close, and if that didn't happen, well then, we're all pretty happy for you. You seem to be a nice enough guy."

The street was dark as he pulled up in front of Robin's house, but he noticed a light on in the front room. He sat in the car for a moment, wondering if he really wanted to tell her about all the weird things that were going on. He might even be too embarrassed to reveal what he discovered about Ginny. He finally decided that he wasn't in the mood to tell Robin his troubles this evening and walked across the street to Susanna's house.

chapter 12

THE RENOVATION WORK that was both a highlight and lowlight in the life of Charlie Wintergreen was eventually completed, and the finished product was put on the market. When he began work on the inherited property, it was all about the house, fixing it up to be resold and spending time with Ginny. Later, he would find it would be more about coming face-to-face with the presence of his niece and trying to understand what she seemed to be asking him to do.

Charlie was devastated after discovering how Susanna and Darla had been treated by his parents, and felt even worse about how their young lives turned out. Heartaches he had known previously during the winter months would pale in comparison to how badly they would be in the future now that he had a real reason to be heartbroken. Deep down, he was hoping if he stayed until the house was sold that he might see his niece again, but she never reappeared, and he was left to wonder about the meaning of it all.

It was as if the vision that appeared to him was only there to point out the obvious, but was that it? Was he only to learn of his sister's life and of his niece's death the way they were both treated by his parents? Finis! The end! No more than that. In his heart, he knew there was more than what he had learned so far. But what could it be? He didn't realize that a child could bring so much joy to his life, even if it was merely a vision of one. He would never forget her laugh when she was with him or that impish smile. The thought of her in his arms would replay in his mind again and again.

The realtor said that the refinished house would probably sell for an amount of money that was so far out of the realm of Charlie's understanding of property values that it shocked him. Money wasn't as important to him now as he thought it would be when he initially arrived in Denver, and he wasn't even considering what he might do with the proceeds from the sale. It was meaningless money to him. The house sold the first week it was on the market, and he closed on the deal two weeks later, and he found both instances to be amazing.

On the day he moved out, he stood in front of the brick home, with its new windows and doors, new roof, and fresh coat of paint, and thought about all that happened to him since he first arrived in the city.

What an experience it had been. Who would have imagined that a good old boy from Grand River would ever have been involved in the things he was, but he was sure wishing that he knew what Darla meant when she told him to love the children. Maybe the answer was waiting for him in Indiana. Maybe that's where Charlie was supposed to love children. Then again, maybe he would spend the rest of his life sitting on a tractor, growing old without ever knowing the meaning of what was asked of him and wondering if he should have stayed in Colorado and continued looking for the answer.

There would be one last look around the property before he left for the airport and the trip back home. His bags were packed, and his plane ticket was in the front pocket of his shirt. It was time to leave, but he wanted to savor the moment, to be able to remember all that he could about the old house that once was home to a part of a family he knew little about. He was proud of what he accomplished while here, and the last few months while he worked on the project had changed him forever.

He opened the car door, and as he was about to enter, something caught his eye, and he looked to the second-floor window, the window in the attic. He caught a glimpse of movement, and when he stared at it long enough, he saw what it was. Standing behind the window, barely visible, was the spirit of Darla. She was waving to him, telling him good-bye. She had that same smile on her face that broke his heart the first time he saw her. It was killing him now. If she was still alive, he wouldn't be leaving like he was, and wasn't certain he could now.

He stood there for a moment, seemingly transfixed by the image in the window. He finally waved back to the little girl, feeling as downtrodden as he had ever been.

"Who you waving to, Charlie?"

Robin had crossed the street when she saw him loading the car, wanting to bid farewell to the man she had grown to like. He quickly looked away from the house as he answered.

"I guess I'm just saying good-bye to all the memories I have of working here on Susanna's house. I'll tell you, Robin, leaving here might just be the hardest thing I've ever done in my life." He glanced at the upstairs window as he spoke, hoping that the image of his niece was still there, but the window was now vacant.

"Then don't go."

He stared silently at her for a moment, trying to tell if she was serious, because he couldn't believe what she seemed to be suggesting. "Stay here?" he finally asked. "Why would I stay? My work is finished, and I have a life in Indiana to go back to."

"Do you? From what you've told me, I don't think you'll be very happy back there."

He decided to seize the opportunity that seemed to be presenting itself and share his story with her, if she would let him.

"Are you busy right now? I'd like to tell you about something that's been on my mind and ask for your input."

There was no hesitation in her voice as there was the first time they met.

"I've got nothing going on today except maybe some house cleaning, and I'm never in a hurry to do that. Let's go have a cup of coffee at my house, but this time, I'm afraid there isn't any cake."

He didn't care about dessert, he told her. He just needed someone to be with and to listen to him.

The inside of her house was tastefully furnished, in a traditional, comfortable way, and Charlie felt immediately at home inside Robin's bungalow. He also felt very much at ease conversing with her about the issues he was faced with, both back home and in Denver, and decided to tell her about what had been occurring inside Susanna's house.

She hung on his every word as he related the goings-on inside the house across the street, with an occasional "Really" or "Oh, my God" thrown into the conversation.

"I do believe you," she told him when he finished the story. "If ever there was a situation where something like that might happen, it would be the tragedy that was Darla's life.

"I'll tell you, Charlie, I didn't know what to make of you the first time I met you. All I knew about your sister was that she was miserable and alone most of her life. Then you show up after she died and start working on her place. I was having a real hard time with that and wasn't certain if you were sincere or just taking advantage of her death to make some money for yourself. But after what you have told me today, and from just being around you a little, I believe you have your sister's best interests at heart."

"I'm just so confused right now. As much as there is a life waiting for me back East, I really don't want to go home and be lonely again. I really don't! These past few months have changed me so much. I want to do something to preserve the memory of everything that has happened, but I don't have a clue as to what that might be. What do you think my niece meant by telling me to love the children?"

She sat there for a moment, thinking about her answer, and finally said, "I'm not certain what she meant, Charlie. I mean, it's so ambiguous that it could take on many different meanings. You might think I'm out of line by suggesting what I'm about to, but I do know of someplace in need of help. It's a place that cares for abandoned and abused children right here in Colorado. I doubt if that's what your niece was alluding to, but it is someplace that needs all the love a person has to give."

"You mean like an orphanage?"

"Well, I don't think there are those kinds of places anymore, except maybe like a Boy's and Girl's Town, but the place I'm talking about sure needs someone to love children who haven't had very much of that in their young lives. I volunteer there whenever I can, but it's in the mountains, a couple of hours' drive from here. Would you like to go with me tomorrow when I drive up there and see for yourself?"

"What would I be doing once we got there?"

"You don't have to do anything but accompany me and just get an idea of the kind of people who are there and see if you think you might be interested in going back again some time."

He didn't have to think about the answer very long, telling her that he would have to cancel his flight and find a place to spend the night but that he would very much like to take the trip into the mountains, an area that seemed to be calling to him again and again.

"I have an extra room if you would like to stay here."

There was a time in the not-to-distant past when Charlie would have looked away from Robin, acting his usual embarrassed self before answering her in a naïve kind of way, but not any longer.

"You sure you wouldn't mind?"

"No, I wouldn't. We have a lot to talk about."

chapter 13

THE TIME DRIVING into the mountains the next day passed quickly as the two occupants of the Ford Explorer talked about the place they were heading to and the work being done there. Charlie wanted to drive so that he would remember the way there in case he might ever want to return.

"Who runs this place and what's it called?" he wanted to know.

"The name of it is Winding Creek House, and it's operated by a non-denominational social service organization out of Denver. It's only been around for a few years, and it's not as organized as I would like it to be, but they're providing a service that is really needed in this area. Don't be too disappointed when you see the place, because it's in need of a lot of tender, loving care, not to mention an awful lot of work. The old, two-story house was donated to the organization by a friend, and it has filled a definite need, but it's only a beginning."

The entire time Robin was talking, Charlie was not only trying to visualize the place she spoke of, but he was already wondering what role he might be able to play there. Was this it? Was Winding Creek House the place he was supposed to be?

"Charlie, things have been pretty rough for you since you arrived in Colorado, so I want you to relax today and just enjoy the ride. You honest-to-God don't have to do anything once we arrive." Robin never looked at Charlie as she spoke, her eyes fixed on the road ahead, but when she turned to see what his response would be, she saw him staring at her as if hanging on every word.

"Let's just see what happens, Robin. I know that I'm supposed to be in the mountains doing something. Maybe it's helping you and the others at this place we're heading to; I don't know. I might not know the answer to that even after spending some time here, but I am enjoying the drive, and especially being alone with you."

She blushed then, bright smile lighting up her face as she continued to enjoy the ride into the high country. Charlie looked at her admiringly.

The black Ford Explorer pulled into the driveway hours after beginning the trip, Robin excited about having Charlie along and him anxious to learn of the work being done there. He was also eager to meet the people helping out at Winding Creek.

The house was nestled among a grove of trees that partially obscured the view from the road. The two-story, brown-shingled structure was almost nondescript, looking very much like a residence one might see anywhere. Paint was peeling off the wood siding and windows.

"This is it! Like I told you, it isn't much to look at, but what's important is what's taking place inside."

Once inside the building, he was introduced to the director, who was a middle-aged woman with straight, white hair. She reminded Charlie of a hippie from the seventies, one of those flower children who lived in a commune and grew their own food in a communal plot of ground. Plain-looking without any makeup, she wore a floor-length simple dress, black Crocs, and no socks.

"Welcome to Winding Creek House, Charlie," she said. "Are you just visiting or were you brought here to work?"

"Well, ma'am, if I said I was here to work, just what is it I would be doing?"

The director's name was Charlotte, and she turned to Robin with a knowing smile before answering. Robin was kind of smiling, too, as if they both knew something that Charlie didn't know.

"Are you planning on staying here for a few hours or a few days?"

She laughed then, and Robin joined in. Charlie didn't know what to think of the dialogue going on around him. *If they want something done*, he thought, *why don't they just ask me?* He reached into his back pocket for his tobacco.

"I thought we were just visiting today, but if there is something I can do while we're here, I'll be glad to help. But first, I wonder if you would mind if I just took a walk around the place. I'd like to see the lay of the land and get my bearings."

"I wouldn't mind at all. There's a dirt path behind the house that leads to a beautiful lookout high on a ridge. It's a somewhat long, difficult climb, but one that's well worth the effort once you get to the top."

He left to walk the pathway, with the women heading to the kitchen to prepare the noontime meal. He glanced at Robin as he reached for the screen door. She was smiling at him in a loving kind of way, and it made him feel good about being with her.

The heavily trodden dirt walkway wound around huge rocks and across green meadows as it made its way higher and higher. Charlie struggled for most of the climb but still found the walk to be exhilarating and exciting. The air was clear and clean-smelling, and wild flowers were in bloom all around him. He loved being outdoors, especially in the higher elevations, and wondered if he could really leave it behind.

Almost an hour passed before the path made a final bend and ended with a view looking west. The sight was spectacular, almost taking away what little breath remained in his lungs. He was so entranced by the beauty around him that he didn't realize he was sharing the scene with another person.

The young girl he saw then was sitting on top of the highest point around them, legs dangling over the drop-off side of the boulder, her eyes fixed beneath her.

"Hi!" he said when he saw her there.

There was no response.

"Are you okay?"

Again, there was no answer as she continued looking straight down.

"My name's Charlie. I've never been here before. Isn't this view the most amazing thing you've ever seen? Maybe because where I'm from, I'm not used to seeing so much beauty. Are you from around here?"

She looked at Charlie then, still not answering his questions, tears filling her young eyes and staining her clothing as they fell down her cheeks.

"Are you hurt?" he wanted to know when he saw the tears. "Is there anything I can do to help you?"

This time she spoke, the words coming out of her trembling mouth in short, hesitant sounds, not much louder than a whisper.

"No," she said. "You can't help me."

"Well, aren't you afraid you might fall off of that cliff you're sitting on, 'cause you're sure scaring the heck out of me sitting there like you are."

She didn't respond but continued sobbing, head bowed until it was almost touching her chest.

"Please leave me alone," she finally said after several moments of silence. "No one can help me. I just want to die." Tears flowed down her young face.

"Listen, young lady, I can't possibly imagine what you are going through right now, but you're obviously in pain over something that has happened to you. I don't want to see you do anything to hurt yourself. So, why don't you just come down here closer to me, and we can talk about whatever you want to talk about."

"No! Go away!" she practically screamed at him.

He moved closer to her location and began speaking in soft, calm tones.

"Can you tell me your name? My name is Charlie. I'll tell you, miss, God has sure made some beautiful scenery for us to look at, hasn't He?"

She didn't respond, but she didn't tell him to go away again either, so he continued talking, thinking he might be able to persuade her to come to a safer place without actually saying the words.

"I'm a farmer from the Midwest. I grow things like corn and beans and wheat, and sometimes mint. Did you ever chew gum that had a spearmint or peppermint taste to it? They use mint like I grow in my fields back home to add that flavor to the gum. You should smell it when it's growing in the fields. There's a sweet aroma in the air so that anyone within a few miles downwind can enjoy it. I just love to work the fields when the sprigs are blooming. I bet you would like it, too."

He moved then, a little closer to the young girl and sat on a nearby round boulder, looking at the view below and hoping she wasn't going to move closer to the edge.

"And in the fall when we harvest the crop, we take it to a nearby still, kind of like where they make illegal booze at, and they turn the crop into a liquid. Then we take the distilled product and put it in drums before shipping it out to a buyer."

"You don't use a still to make mint. It just grows. I've seen leaves of mint and they weren't liquid."

Charlie was relieved to have her answer him, thinking that it would help take her mind off what she was thinking about doing.

"Yeah, there are leaves of mint, too, but what companies use in their products to give it a minty aroma and taste is in a liquid form. Have you ever been on a farm?"

She looked at him for a while before answering.

"No."

"I've got me a pretty big place back in Indiana, nearly one thousand acres of dirt fields that I plant crops on every year. It's hard work. But I kind of enjoy it."

"Do you have any kids?" She was talking now, and he thought that was a good sign.

"I've never been married, but my sister had a little girl, and she was the cutest little thing you ever saw."

She had stopped crying and seemed to be listening to what he was saying.

"Did you ever hit her?" she asked.

He couldn't believe she would even ask a question like that. Was it because someone had been abusing her?

"I've never hit a child or anyone else in my life, and I sure wouldn't have hit my niece. I believe children are God's gift to us, and I'm sorry it took me so long to realize that. Like I said, I've never been married so I don't have any children of my own, and I'm sure sorry about that now."

"My dad has hit me for as long as I can remember, and when he does, he tells me it's because I'm no good and I deserve to be punished."

"Is your dad with you here?"

"No."

"Let me tell you, young lady. No one is going to hit you while I'm here. I promise you that. No one is going to hurt you. I just won't let them. What do you say you and I walk back down to the house and get a bite to eat?"

"I can't."

"Why not?"

"I'm afraid to move. I'm afraid I'm going to fall off if I move from here."

He got up then and climbed up to where she was and held out his hand.

"Take my hand."

"No! I'm afraid to move."

With some effort, he got on top of the boulder where she was sitting and scooted closer to her side. *No wonder she's scared*, he thought as he could now see what she was looking at. It was enough to turn a girl's curly hair straight. He continued moving closer to her until they were touching.

"Is it okay if I hold on to your arm? I'm going to start moving backwards away from the ledge, and I want you to move with me. Okay?"

She didn't answer, and for the first time, he could tell there was an absolute look of terror on her face. He decided to try moving her with him as he scooted backwards away from danger. He held on to her arm tightly and began moving slowly. She followed without saying a word. They continued on, inch by inch, for what seemed like an eternity, until he felt it was all right to try and stand. He gently pulled her up with him to the standing position, and when he did, she threw her arms around him and sobbed uncontrollably.

"You're safe now," he said. "You're safe."

Charlie's heart was beating so fast he thought it might leap out of his chest. He didn't want the girl to know how frightened he was, but between his heart racing wildly and her body shaking like an Aspen tree on a mountain top, it was pretty obvious there was fear present.

"What do you say we go back to the house? I believe the women are fixing lunch. Would you like to get something to eat?"

She had stopped crying and was looking at Charlie so sorrowfully that he almost wanted to hold her in his arms forever.

"Are you going there, too?" she wanted to know.

"You bet I am. I'm so hungry I could eat the south end of a north-bound skunk."

She laughed, and Charlie laughed with her, and they started back down the trail that had brought them together.

Just as they turned to begin the trek back down from the mountain top, Robin and Charlotte emerged from around a bend in the path, a look of panic on both their faces. They both looked breathless as if the hike was more than a little difficult for them, and they let out a cry when they saw the young girl.

"Jenny," they cried in unison. "Are you all right?"

The young girl didn't say anything but ran into Charlotte's waiting arms.

Robin moved out of the young girl's way and closer to Charlie.

"Is she okay?" Robin wanted to know.

"I believe she is now, but if you would have seen her a few minutes ago, you wouldn't have thought so."

"We noticed Jenny was missing shortly after you left the house. She's been very despondent over recent events in her life, and we've been keeping a close eye on her, but when we arrived, she must have gone out the back door. I'm not certain what she is capable of doing, but we knew we had to find her," said Robin.

Jenny and Charlotte were leading the way back toward Winding Creek House, Charlotte with her arm around the young girl, while Charlie and Robin walked back slowly so they could continue their conversation.

After Charlie related the story about the girl he now knew to be Jenny, Robin told him he probably saved her life.

"I don't think she was going to jump, but she put herself in such a bad situation that she might have fallen trying to get off of the boulder," he said.

"Regardless, if you hadn't been there, who knows what might have happened."

"What do you know about the girl?" he asked.

"I know she's like all the rest of the children who spend time at Winding Creek House; they've all had a pretty bad life so far, and they usually don't trust adults when they first arrive. We just try to show them that not all grown-ups are like the bad ones they've known."

Going down the mountain trail was a lot easier than the trip up it, and the hike in the fresh air and the events of the morning so far had energized Charlie.

"What is it I can do to help around here?"

Robin stopped and looked at him for a moment, a knowing smile on her face. Charlie would be the right man for this place, as everything that had happened to him since he had been in Colorado had pointed him in this direction.

"Whether you realize it or not, you've already started helping. Now, let's go down to the house and have something to eat. Afterwards, we can all sit down and talk about what your role here might be."

Love the children, my niece told me, *and I didn't have a clue as to what she was talking about*, Charlie thought. *I guess loving comes in many forms, sometimes as simple as not hurting anyone. I haven't known a lot of love myself in my lifetime and have never had much of an opportunity to give any, so maybe this is my chance. Maybe this is what I've been destined to do all my life and just didn't know it until Darla showed me the way. I hope she's looking down at me right now, proud of the journey that I'm about to embark on. If this is what she meant by loving the children, I'm going to give it all I have; if it isn't, maybe she will appear to me again and help me figure it out. In the meantime, there is work to be done here, and I'm eager to begin. And I'm pretty excited about spending more time with Robin.*

They continued walking the mountain trail hand-in-hand, Charlie with a clearer vision of what fate had in store for him.